Praise for
Powerless and Irrelevant

"Powerful and timely book"

This powerful and timely book, *Powerless and Irrelevant: How society sees the Church and how to radically change that view*, offers a deeply insightful and courageous examination of the Church's present spiritual crisis within times of hardship. The author reveals how the Church's perceived irrelevance isn't just because of a chaotic world, but because we've unknowingly mixed the Old and New Covenants together in ways that have led us to a misconception that drains our power and clarity on God's word.

It explains why Bible interest is rising yet church attendance is low, and explores a generation hungering for hope, truth and meaning behind what's being preached within our churches worldwide. The author unpacks this paradox with compassion and deep biblical insight.

The way theological truths are explained is both profound and easy to understand. It challenged me to rethink how I approach God not through performance, but through the fullness of grace offered in Christ.

A must-read for any Christian daring to ask, not just what the church should do - but what the church must become.

—**James Hodgkin**, Anglican Churches Worship Leader, *London UK*

***

"A lucid, well-argued, and ordered account of the problems that beset the Church"

Powerless and Irrelevant – that is what the author, Niall Walshe, believes is society's view of the Church. He states this perception is fair and correct, mainly because many congregations and denominations have absorbed Old Covenant thinking, beliefs, and practices, into the life of the New Covenant.

In its' efforts to maintain old wineskins, Mr. Walshe proposes that the Church's witness is necessarily confused, undermined and ineffective.

Drawing on his many years of experience as an evangelist and church leader, the author is not content to simply explore the problem but thankfully offers a solution. Passionately extolling the enormity and availability of God's grace, Mr. Walshe invites believers to live wholly in the New Covenant and encourages us to examine our understanding of the Bible, so that we can launch out in faith, ready to receive God's promised blessing.

This statement of hope in Jesus and His redeeming work is a liberating call to the many who struggle with doubts and uncertainty.

The book is a lucid, well-argued, and ordered account of the problems that beset the historical and contemporary Church. There are copious and appropriate references to Scripture. It examines modern teaching and practice, raising questions that are answered through biblical quotation.

Aspects of Old and New Covenants are compared in every section, with a helpful conclusion that summarises each chapter. Mr. Walshe urges us not to be satisfied with stumbling along in our walk with God, and instead to live in the knowledge and experience of the grace, standing, and authority, that our relationship with Him confers.

—**Dr Paul Dakin**, Methodist preacher, Former member Pioneer Ministries Forum

"Essential reading for regular churchgoers"

This book, *Powerless and Irrelevant...* is essential reading for regular churchgoers, especially for those who have grown-up in the Church. It is not a book can be simply read and put away; it is a book that needs to be worked through together with the Scriptures.

This book could appear quite radical, and controversial to religious people, but so too was the New Covenant Gospel of God's grace the Apostle Paul was tasked with proclaiming, as is seen in his ministry.

This book challenges the form of Christianity that has become normalised in the lives of many Christians and churches and has the potential to change the widely held perception of the Christian message.

—**Sahan Thalayasingam**, Ministry Team, *St. Mark's Church, Finsbury, London UK*

"Teaches a more accurate understanding of many of the Scriptures"

Niall Walshe's teachings on grace - received many years ago and now clearly laid out in *Powerless and Irrelevant...* radically transformed me. Niall's teachings showed me then that, in the 15 years since becoming a Christian, I had become judgmental and lost my first love.

Powerless and Irrelevant... teaches a more accurate understanding of many of the Scriptures that I, like most Christians, thought I already knew so well.

This deeper understanding of grace, and clearer understanding of what Jesus taught, resulted in the judgementalism fading, and my first love being rekindled. This led to pastoral, prison and evangelistic ministries, and a greater love for the lost.

As the book details how the Church has strayed from its intended path, my heart is stirred to see it return to all that God intended it to be.

I thoroughly recommend *Powerless and Irrelevant…* to anyone who wants deeper understanding of God's empowering grace, wants greater understanding of what Jesus taught, and who longs for the Church to be renewed, revived and empowered.

—**Gilly Ridout**, Deacon, *Willows Community Church, Torquay, Devon UK*

Powerless And Irrelevant

How society sees the Church,
and how to radically change that view

Niall Walshe

Published by KHARIS PUBLISHING, imprint of KHARIS MEDIA LLC.

Copyright © 2025 Niall Walshe

ISBN-13: 978-1-63746-367-3

ISBN-10: 1-63746-367-7

Library of Congress Control Number: 2025945878

All KHARIS PUBLISHING products are available at special quantity discounts for bulk purchases for sales promotions, premiums, fund-raising, and educational needs. For details, contact:

Kharis Media LLC
Tel: 1-630-909-3405
support@kharispublishing.com
www.kharispublishing.com

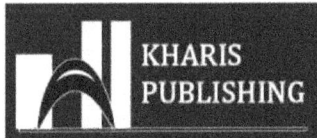

About Niall Walshe

I became a Christian by reading the Bible while working in Saudi Arabia in 1983/4. Returning to the UK in June 1986, I joined the local church in Devon, but within a year, I was in London creating/running a 12-year ministry which included taking young homeless people off the streets of London.

This work was greatly blessed by the Lord, resulting in many young people becoming Christians. It was a time of healing and other miracles, Divine provision (12 years of provision without ever asking anyone for anything) and Divine protection. It was during this work that I had the amazing experience of meeting and sitting, for just one day, under the teaching of Dr. Kenneth E. Bailey. Truly a day that changed my life!

Throughout the homeless work, I preached and taught in churches in London, the Home Counties, and Devon. I presented whole-day teaching events in various locations, majoring on the topic of grace, and the teaching of the Scriptures without the usual cultural overlays and unquestioning acceptance of traditional teachings – leaving the message that Jesus intended to be heard by the first-century peasant folk who were there listening to Him.

While running the homeless work, I led two mission teams aiding an orphanage in Zimbabwe and was part of missions to Romania, Russia, and Sri Lanka – all of which were fruit-bearing.

Returning to secular work in 1999, I still regularly preached and taught in London and Devon.

In 2001 Pentland Press published a book I wrote entitled, "Whatever Happened to the *Good* News?" I have included some testimonials that accompanied the book.

"Niall Walshe's book 'Whatever Happened to the Good News' is a challenging and prophetic word for the Church and all Christians longing for a way out of failure. Is it possible that the contemporary Church is more akin to the Pharisees than the disciples of Jesus? I think the book is important and prophetic."

The late Reverend **Rob Frost**. *Methodist evangelist, author, broadcaster, founder of SEED Teams & Easter People*

"I was introduced to Niall several years ago and sat under his excellent teaching on grace - a subject that very few seem to have a correct understanding of. That night I left with a copy of Niall's book "*Whatever Happened to the Good News*." A couple of days later I was in my garden reading the book when my phone rang. It was hard for me to speak as I was sobbing my heart out because of the truth being revealed to me."

John Gurr, *Surrey*

"I have to say, without seeming over the top, that "*Whatever Happened to the Good News*" is the best Christian book on grace (outside of the Bible itself) that I have ever read. After 16 years, I still have it in my possession and to date have read it 5 times! I also use it for reference purposes from time to time as, to me, it seems to lend itself to this also.

"*Whatever Happened to the Good News*" is a truly wonderful book, bringing to light the grace of God that the Church, churches and the world need to hear about

Nick and Pauline Lambert, *Orgiva, Spain*

Returning to live in Devon (2003), I started a Fellowship which, as part of its ministry, provided two services each month for those incarcerated in Dartmoor Prison. During this ministry, we were blessed with healing miracles within the Fellowship, and some prisoners at Dartmoor became Christians.

In 2005 I started a Facebook-based Christian outreach. The Page, called Christian Truth Today, was blessed by the Lord and had over 10,000 followers, with a good number from closed countries where the Bible is forbidden. This page led to the following invites:

1. In 2006, I undertook a solo trip to Nepal, where I taught at the Manapur Bible School in Hetauda.

2. In 2008, I led a mission team to Uganda, preaching and teaching in the town of Kaliro, a rural location in the north-east of Kampala.

3. In 2009, I returned to Uganda with a co-worker to create a pilot project aimed at achieving self-sufficiency to rural villages – remaining there until

the project was successfully concluded in 2011. Throughout, we preached and taught many Church leaders in Uganda and Kenya.

Since 2022, I have been working on a second book *"Powerless and Irrelevant."*

I have written the book because the Church has absorbed, and now teaches, many doctrinal errors and unbiblical practises, but that situation can be reversed. The message of the book, essentially, is how to reclaim the Gospel as Jesus meant it to be understood by those who were there listening to Him.

I wrote the book because my learning, at a deeper level than usual, about the riches of God's grace and the Gospel message that Jesus taught ran alongside the homeless work where I experienced, encountered and administered God's grace on countless occasions. I saw very damaged young lives restored, healed, and set free by the receiving of Biblical truths. Many of the young homeless people became Christians. Through preaching and teaching opportunities across the years, and in various countries, I have seen that same grace manifested – again, on countless occasions.

The message the Church preaches and teaches today is essentially powerless. It, as 2 Timothy 3:5 expresses it, has, *"...a form of godliness but denying its power."* Tragically, many Christians go through their entire Christian life without ever seeing the supernatural manifest in and through their own lives.

This book identifies the reasons behind this powerlessness and accompanying irrelevance, and shows how that situation can be radically changed, empowering individual Christians and the wider Church to, once again, reveal in this world the truth, the power, the love, compassion and wisdom of Jesus.

I have a passion to see the Church empowered in this way and this book is part of my contribution to try and help that process.

Contents

Part One: How the Church got into this situation 13

The Church has a problem 14

The cause of the Church's problem 15

Some of what has been lost to Christians today 19

The good news 21

Part Two: Doctrines of Christianity 22

Chapter 1 The foundational doctrine of Christianity: A New Covenant ...23

Chapter 2 The doctrine of grace 41

_Part 1: Understanding grace 42

_Part 2: Secure in grace 49

Chapter 3 The doctrine of repentance 56

Chapter 4 The doctrine of forgiveness 67

Chapter 5 The doctrine of righteousness 80

Chapter 6 The doctrine of obedience 94

Chapter 7 The doctrine of sin 111

Part Three: Some commonly mistaught Scriptures 123

Introduction 124

Part Four: Unbiblical practices in Church 140

Introduction 141

Part Five: The way forward 161

"As of first importance…" 162

Part One:

How the Church got into this situation

The Church has a problem

It's the mid-2020s. The world is in a mess. We are living through a time of increased wars and rumours of war. Europe is witnessing its largest conflict since World War 2, and with every possibility that it will develop into an even larger conflagration. The Middle East continues to bubble away, conflict and terror attacks never further away than just below the surface, ready to erupt at any moment. In Asia, if the fragile standoff between China and Taiwan results in a Chinese invasion of Taiwan, the world could be facing the onset of World War III. This is due to the USA's treaty obligation to defend Taiwan in the event of an attack by China.

Apart from war, famines are increasing around the world. Poverty is increasing. Diseases are increasing in number and severity. Natural events such as earthquakes are increasing.

But those issues are not the problem that the Church has.

At national levels, even the once wealthy "Western world" is seeing dramatic declines in standards of living amidst increasing poverty. In many of the western nations, basic infrastructure including health provision, education provision, transport links (roads and rail), care for the elderly and sick, housing, law and order provision, and all aspects of Governmental provision for the meeting of societal needs are in steady decline.

Globally, multitudes of people are living with increasing fear, and hopelessness, with little peace or sense of purpose and meaning in their lives.

But those issues are not the problem that the Church has.

In the USA in 2024, Bible sales increased by 22%, resulting in millions of additional Bibles being sold. A similar trend was observed in the UK. In both countries, the majority of buyers were young people from Gen Z, which includes those in their early teenage years to those in their late twenties.

That sounds like great news. And it is. Millions of young adults, likely not just in the US and the UK are turning to the Bible for answers amid global instability. They seek reassurance, peace, hope, meaning, and purpose in their lives. The increase in Bible sales has presented a challenge for the Church. Despite this rise, there has not been a similar increase in church attendance in either the US or the UK. Young adults are turning to the Bible for answers and support, but they do not view the Church as part of the solution.

And THAT is the problem the Church now has.

Amidst the greatest global instability since the end of World War 2, the general mass of the public in countries around the world sees the Church as, essentially, powerless and irrelevant in the face of unprecedented global, societal and personal needs and fears.

The Church must, first, face that truth. It is seen as powerless and irrelevant. Then, it must examine itself honestly to understand how, after 2,000 years, we have found ourselves in this situation.

That necessary examination is provided in this book.

The cause of the Church's problem

There is one very simple reason the Church is ignored by most people even in the current dire situations around the globe. It is that…

…for 2,000 years the Church has slowly and, it is to be hoped, without realising it, absorbed Old Covenant doctrines and practices into the New Covenant.

That is the primary reason the Church is now regarded as powerless and irrelevant.

We need to examine and understand why incorporating some Old Covenant laws, doctrines, and practices into the New Covenant despite both being the Word of God, can have such a devastating impact on Christian witness and influence in society.

Reason 1: No Biblical mandate

(a) Christians have not understood, or have ignored, several teachings in the New Testament about mixing the Old and New Covenants.

The first teaching to examine is one from Jesus in Matthew 9:14- 17. In this passage Jesus tells a parable and, in keeping with understanding all parables, it is necessary to look back to just before Jesus tells the parable to identify what question or issue, He is responding to through the parable.

The key to understanding this parable in Matthew 9 is the question asked by the disciples of John in verse 14: *Then John's disciples came and asked Him, "How is it that we and the Pharisees fast often, but Your disciples do not fast?"*

John's disciples were not against Jesus or trying to catch Him out in His answer, as the Pharisees often tried to do. It was John, the teacher of this group of his followers, who declared of Jesus, in John 1:29, *"Look, the Lamb of God, who takes away the sin of the world!"*

So, these men were not out to trap Jesus, they were just genuinely puzzled. The Old Covenant – the Covenant of Moses – required regular fasting, Jesus was a recognised teacher, yet He appeared to be ignoring the Old Covenant and the Law. How could these two truths be reconciled?

It is in response to this question that Jesus tells what has become known as the parable of the wineskins:

"Jesus answered, "How can the guests of the bridegroom mourn while he is with them? The time will come when the bridegroom will be taken from them; then they will fast. No one sews a patch of unshrunk cloth on an old garment, for the patch will pull away from the garment, making the tear worse. Neither do people pour new wine into old wineskins. If they do, the skins will burst; the wine will run out and the wineskins will be ruined. No, they pour new wine into new wineskins, and both are preserved."

Jesus is making two points in that response. The first point is that He is declaring that He is bringing in a new Covenant, a new law. He is not here to simply reinforce the old Law of Moses. The second point is that He explains what will happen if people try and mix the two Covenants.

In His parable, the wineskins burst and the new wine spills out.

The wineskins were already old, and now they have burst open and are ruined. They will not be used again. The wine has spilled out onto the ground. It cannot be recovered.

In short, the mixing of old and new creates something that is of no use to anyone for anything.

That is the situation in the Church today because of the mixing of the Old Covenant and the New Covenant. The Church has ended up with something that is of no use to anyone. So, even in dire times, people do not turn to the Church for answers, direction and help.

Just realising the Church has ignored, or at least not understood, a teaching from Jesus, and is doing the thing He expressly taught would be very harmful and disempowering, immediately highlights why the Church has become powerless and irrelevant to societies around the world today.

(b) A related question arose amongst early Christian when, as described in Acts 15, some Jewish believers insisted that new Gentile believers should be circumcised. The issue caused much debate and led to a group of believers, led by Paul and Barnabas, being authorised to go to Jerusalem to seek an answer from the Apostles and Elders there.

After much discussion, the Apostles and Elders agreed and declared through Peter, Acts 15:10-11, *"Now then, why do you try to test God by putting on the necks of Gentiles a yoke that neither we nor our ancestors have been able to bear? No! We believe it is through the grace of our Lord Jesus that we are saved, just as they are."*

That decision and declaration ended the practice of trying to force circumcision on Gentile believers. However, for 2,000 years the Church appears to have missed the wider point under discussion at that Council of Jerusalem.

Was it simply a discussion about circumcision? Or was it a debate about the whole of the Old Covenant in relation to believers in Christ? James provides the answer to that question when he writes, in James 2:10, *"For whoever keeps the whole law and yet stumbles at just one point is guilty of breaking all of it."*

So, the Apostles and Elders could not simply "delete" the law about circumcision if the rest of the Law remained in force. It is an either/or situation. Either the Law is still in force and, therefore new believers, by that Law must be circumcised and keep the rest of the Law as well, or circumcision – and therefore the remainder of the Law – does not apply to Christian believers.

With this understanding, it becomes immediately obvious that there is no Biblical mandate for Christians to absorb any aspects of Old Covenant Law or doctrines.

(c) Other illustrations of how the Old Covenant, the Law of Moses, is inapplicable to Christians are given through various Scriptures including Psalm 147:19-20, *"He has revealed His word to Jacob, His laws and decrees to Israel. He has done this for no other nation; they do not know His laws."* Paul refers to this truth in Romans 2:14 when he is speaking of the Gentiles and writes, *"Indeed when Gentiles who do not have the Law..."* That declaration makes it clear that the Law (the Old Covenant) was not given to the Gentiles.

(d) Paul, in Galatians 3 whilst discussing whether salvation is by faith or by obeying the Law, makes it clear that no one can add or take away from a duly established Covenant – meaning that, as the Gentiles were not included in the Law when it was originally given to Moses and Israel, Gentiles can at no point simply add themselves into that Covenant nor take parts of the Old Covenant and add them to the New Covenant.

Taking the points made above, it is very clear that any adherence by a Christian to the laws or doctrines of the Old Covenant has no Biblical mandate whatsoever and therefore puts that adherent outside of the will of God, and God will not, cannot, bless and work through such a person in such a position.

Reason 2 – A changed relationship with God

The Old Covenant and the New Covenant stand in opposition in many ways. Both Covenants established how a relationship with God could be established and sustained by those under their respective Covenants.

So, for example, when Moses ascended the mountain to receive the Law of the Old Covenant from God, God instructed Moses to first (Exodus 19:24), *"Go down and bring Aaron up with you. But the priests and the people must not force their way through to come up to the Lord, or He will break out against them."* It was always going to be a distant relationship, and one based on obedience.

On the other hand, in the New Covenant, the Christian is told, (Romans 8:15), *"The Spirit you received does not make you slaves so that you live in fear again; rather, the Spirit you received brought about your adoption to sonship. And by Him, we cry, "Abba, Father.""* Not a distant relationship, but now a family relationship.

In the Old Covenant, obedience determined God's blessings upon the individual, (Deuteronomy 28:2), *"All these blessings will come on you and accompany you if you obey the Lord your God."*

In contrast, in the New Covenant, (John 1:16), *"Out of the fullness of His grace we have all received one blessing after another."*

There are countless contrasts that exist between the Old and New Covenants, but one simple understanding of the fundamental difference between the Old and New Covenants will also help Christians understand why mixing the Covenants will change their relationship with God.

The fundamental difference is this: the Old Covenant is all about people doing things for God, and the New Covenant is all about God doing things for humanity. When Christians accept aspects of the Old Covenant in their relationship with God it becomes, as is the whole of the Old Covenant, a performance-based relationship.

So, the question every Christian must ask of themselves to understand whether they are living fully under the New Covenant or whether they are living with a mix of both Covenants is: "Am I working for God, or am I simply receiving what I do not deserve from God, or am I doing a mixture of both?"

Some of what has been lost to Christians today

(a), <u>Peace with God</u>. Living with a mixture of Old and New Covenant doctrines and practices robs Christians of the peace that should be theirs in their relationship with God. Romans 5:1, *"Therefore, since we have been justified through faith, we have peace with God through our Lord Jesus Christ…"* Mixing the Old and New Covenants may lead Christians to believe they are justified by faith and works. However, when they rely on their own works, they may lose peace in their relationship with God. This is because Christians will always fall short of who they aspire to be and what they mistakenly think God expects from them. That lack of peace will then hinder their Christian witness.

Without that peace in their relationship with God, will a Christian have the faith and confidence to lay hands on a person and pray for healing? Probably not, because they will struggle to believe God will use them.

(b) <u>The ability to stand</u> (not be overcome by the enemy). Romans 5:2, *"…we have gained access by faith into this grace in which we now stand."* By grace, by faith, Christians can stand against all the enemy and this world has to throw at them. But when faith is mixed with works, and grace is mixed with Law, Christians lose confidence in their standing before God, allowing the enemy and/or the world to overcome them. Doubts, fears, lack of confidence and similar emotions and thoughts, often arise when we lose our ability to stand firm. This can ultimately diminish the effectiveness of our Christian witness.

(c) <u>Security from enemy attack</u>. Ephesians 6:14, *"…the breastplate of righteousness…"* Mixing the Covenants leads at times to Christians looking to their own earned "righteousness" (which, of course, is never good enough) rather than relying entirely upon the God-given righteousness of the New Covenant, thus allowing the enemy a route by which to attack them. Knowing how God sees them – as righteous in Christ – gives the Christian confidence in God's support through the tough times. Without that confidence, the Christian may well back away from whatever challenge the enemy has put in front of them, thus eliminating the Christian witness.

(d) <u>Power to overcome</u>. Ephesians 6:16, *"…take up the shield of faith, with which you can extinguish all the flaming arrows of the evil one."* When faith, mixed with works from different Covenants, is combined, Christians lose the protective power that comes through the shield of faith. The power to overcome everything the enemy has. Without that shield in place, the Christian is significantly more vulnerable to physical, emotional and spiritual attacks from the enemy.

(e) <u>An effective prayer life</u>. James 5:16 says, *"The prayer of a righteous person is powerful and effective."* A Christian living with a mixture of Old and New Covenants teachings on righteousness will, at times, doubt their right standing (their righteousness) before God and this, through lack of faith and a sense of unworthiness, will lead to a powerless and ineffective prayer life.

(f) <u>God's help in every situation</u>. Hebrews 4:16, *"Let us then approach God's throne of grace with confidence, so that we may receive mercy and find grace to help us in our time of need."* God stands ready to help His children in every situation. When, however, grace is muddied by Law, and through a self-perceived sense of unworthiness that accompanies the mixing of the Covenants, the Christian will often hold back from approaching God in their time of need, let alone approaching God *"...with confidence..."* that He will meet their needs at that point. The Christian loses the opportunity to manifest Christ in this world, believing themselves unworthy.

The list of all that has been lost by Christians who live with a mixture of Old and New Covenants is longer, but even from the short list above it can be seen how so much power and effectiveness has been lost by the Christian Church.

The good news

The reality of the Church today, perceived by the vast majority (even from within its own ranks) as powerless and irrelevant, may appear somewhat bleak. The good news, however, is that the situation within the Church, and therefore the perception of the Church by the general public, can be restored to what it Biblically should be.

Christians need only to understand properly the New Covenant, identify and remove any Old Covenant doctrines and/or practices from their understanding of Christianity, and then live as Christians fully under the New Covenant.

Part Two

Doctrines of Christianity

Chapter 1

The foundational doctrine of Christianity: A New Covenant

The Bible is divided into two parts – the Old Testament and the New Testament. The word "testament" means "covenant," which in turn means "agreement." So, in modern terminology, the Bible is divided into two parts – the Old Agreement and the New Agreement. The "Agreement" is the Old Agreement between God and Israel, and the New Agreement between God and humanity. The Old Agreement outlines how Israel would maintain a relationship with God, whereas the New Agreement outlines how all humanity, individually, may enter into a relationship with God, a relationship that will endure for all eternity.

The lack of proper understanding of the Bible's teachings over many centuries - which has led to mis-teaching of the Bible up to and including the present day, with the resultant decline in Biblical Christianity - stems from a supposed dilemma that the Church, both the various organised denominations and the individual Christian, has for the most part still not resolved.

The supposed dilemma is this: <u>What does the Church do with the Old Agreement now that there is a New Agreement</u>? The problem for the Church is that it, correctly, sees the whole of the Bible as God's Word and to abandon or reject the Old Agreement seems synonymous with abandoning or rejecting swathes of God's inspired Word - His teachings, His commands, His promises and so on.

The Church's solution has been to blend the Old and New Agreements. The problem for the Church, though, and for individual Christians, is that the two Agreements are irreconcilable, and many of the doctrines in the New Agreement stand opposed to doctrines in the Old Agreement. The Church's attempted "blending" of the two Agreements, and the resultant confusion and mis-teaching, affects all the major doctrines of Christianity – grace, repentance, forgiveness, obedience, righteousness - as well as teachings on Christian living.

This issue of opposing doctrines starts with the most fundamental doctrine in each Agreement and that is: how an individual is saved from God's punishment for their sins and brought into a relationship with God. The Old Agreement teaches that it is through individual effort by each Israelite through obedience to the Law – which led only to a limited relationship, whereas the New Agreement teaches that it is through God's grace freely offered that every individual in the world may enter into an eternal relationship.

If the supposed dilemma of what to do with the Old Agreement is resolved that will beneficially impact the understanding of all the doctrines of Christianity and allow for a more accurate application of the message of the New Agreement, and the Bible overall. It is this issue of resolving the dilemma of what to do with the Old Agreement, thus enabling a Christian to live fully under New Agreement doctrines, that will now be addressed.

Separating the Agreements

Colossians 1:6 says, *"All over the world this Gospel is bearing fruit and growing, just as it has been doing among you **since the day you** heard it and **understood God's grace** in all its truth."* Only when God's grace – revealed in the New Agreement – is both heard <u>and</u> understood does the New Agreement grow and bear fruit. This growth and fruit result from Biblical Christianity, requiring Christians to separate themselves from the Old Agreement and fully embrace God's grace.

Some differences between the two Agreements are set out below. They illustrate how the two Agreements are fundamentally incompatible, and how attempting to blend them together will always create the confusion and ineffectiveness that epitomises modern-day Christianity.

Old Agreement		New Agreement	
Law	Ex 24:12	Grace	Titus 3:7
Israel only	Rom 2:14	For all humanity	Jn 3:16
Works	Dt 6:25	Faith	Eph 2:8
Conditional blessings	Dt 28:1-2	Unconditional blessings	Jn 1:16
Limited in time	Gal 3:19	Eternal	Heb 13:20
Earned righteousness	Rom 9:31	Gift of righteousness	Rom 5:17
Held people prisoner	Gal 3:23	Sets people free	Heb 9:15
Lower standard	Matt 5:21	Higher standard	Matt 5:22
A shadow of reality	Heb 10:1	Reality	Col 2:17
A distant relationship	Ex 19:24	Family relationship	Rom 8:15
		Unaffected by Moses	Gal 3:17

The differences explained

1a. Old Agreement: Law

The Old Agreement is centred on the Law of Moses including teachings on forgiveness, repentance, obedience and other issues fundamental to Christianity. It is an Agreement rooted in all the laws (hundreds of them, not just the Ten Commandments) given by God to the people of Israel through Moses.

Obedience to the Law makes a relationship with God possible, and the blessings received depend upon it. A system of repentance and sacrifice was instituted to cover any disobedience.

1b. New Agreement: Grace

The New Agreement is centred on the person of Jesus Christ – His birth, life, death, and resurrection. It is an Agreement rooted in grace and faith. The Christian's relationship with God does not depend upon countless rules and regulations, it does not depend upon the Christian doing something for God but, instead, depends upon God doing something for humanity.

Titus 3:7 says, *"...having been justified by His grace, we might become heirs having the hope of eternal life."* Christians are made right with God through His grace. That is the fundamental truth, the Good News, of the New Covenant, the New Agreement. The Christian's secure, eternal relationship with God has nothing to do with their own effort.

2a. <u>Old Agreement</u>: Between God and Israel only

The Old Agreement (Law of Moses) was given to Israel, and Israel alone. Psalm 147:19-20 says, *"He (God) has revealed His Word to Jacob, His Laws and decrees to Israel. He has done this for no other nation; they do not know His Laws."* Paul writes in Romans 2:14, *"Indeed when Gentiles who do not have The Law..."* - making clear that The Law was not given to the Gentiles (non-Jews). When writing about Israel, Paul says, Romans 9:4, *"...the people of Israel. Theirs is the adoption as sons; theirs the divine glory, the covenants, the receiving of The Law..."*

The Law, the Old Agreement, was never given to anyone except Israel.

2b. <u>New Agreement</u>: Universal, for all nations and every individual

On the other hand, the Covenant of Christ – the New Agreement - was offered to the whole world - to Jews and Gentiles alike. John 3:16, *"For God so loved the world that He gave His one and only Son that <u>whoever</u> believes in Him shall not perish but have eternal life."* Now the whole world is offered reconciliation with God, now the whole world is offered salvation. There is no need to try and add the Gentiles to the Covenant of Moses for now there is a Covenant for Gentiles and Jews alike. It is a Covenant, an Agreement, for which there is a Biblical mandate; it is the Covenant of Christ, the New Agreement.

Summary of this second difference

This one difference proves beyond doubt that not applying the Old Agreement to Christians is the Biblical thing to do – and does not involve abandoning or rejecting any of God's Word but, rather, adhering to it.

There is not one verse in the Bible to suggest that The Law, including the Ten Commandments, was ever given, or extended, to the Gentiles – to non-Israelites. It was given to Israel, and it remained with Israel. It is an error that the Ten Commandments (being part of the Law of the Old Agreement) have become such a central pillar of the Christian church when they were never given to anyone except the Jewish nation of Israel.

The Christian church has taken on something to which it has no right. In Galatians 3:15 Paul writes that no one can add or take away from a duly established covenant. God established the Covenant of Moses, consisting of the Law of Moses, with Israel. No one can add the Gentiles simply because it seems a good code of moral living - nor, indeed, for any other reason. The Covenant of Moses was never intended for, nor given to the Gentiles.

This is such an important point because those who argue in favour of adherence to the Ten Commandments (or any other aspects of The Law) as Christian guidance have no Biblical mandate and are teaching and acting contrary to the Word of God – contrary to Biblical Christianity.

The crucial problem for the Christian created by the introduction of any obligation to obey aspects of the Law is that it changes the basis of the Christian's relationship with God – from grace to grace + Law, from faith to faith + works. And so on.

3a. <u>Old Agreement</u>: Individual and collective obedience

The Covenant of Moses was an Agreement under which God called Israel into a relationship with Himself based strictly on their individual and collective obedience. Moses says in Deuteronomy 28, *"If you fully obey the Lord your God and carefully follow all His commands I give you today, the Lord your God will set you high above all the nations on earth. All these blessings will come upon you and accompany you if you obey the Lord your God..."* The other side of the coin is that if Israel is disobedient, in that same chapter Moses says, *"However, if you do not obey the Lord your God and do not carefully follow all His commands and decrees I am giving you today, all these curses will come upon you and overtake you..."* God says these curses include: *"I will curse you in the fields and I will curse you in the cities, I will curse you in your womb. I will curse you in your crops. I will hand you over to your enemies."* If Israel fails to follow His Law, every aspect of life will be subject to God's curse.

The prophet Daniel later declares, in Daniel 9:11, *"All Israel has transgressed Your Law, and turned away, refusing to obey You. Therefore, the curses and sworn judgments written in the Law of Moses, the servant of God, have been poured out on us because we have sinned against You."* So, what God said, God meant! "If you do not obey Me, I will curse you."

3b. New Agreement: Faith

The New Agreement, in Christ, is a covenant of faith – Ephesians 2:8, *"For it is by grace you have been saved, through faith. And this is not of yourselves, it is the gift of God."* Under the New Agreement, every individual is called to believe in the Bible's teaching about Jesus. That belief, that faith in Jesus, ensures a secure, eternal relationship with God. John 3:18, *"Whoever believes in Him is not condemned, but whoever does not believe stands condemned already because they have not believed in the name of God's one and only Son."* And, as Ephesians 2:8 teaches, God gives Christians the faith they need to believe. It is all a work of God for humanity.

4a. <u>Old Agreement</u>: Conditional blessings

In Deuteronomy 28:2 Moses says to Israel, *"All these blessings will come upon you and accompany you if you obey the Lord your God..."* Blessings followed obedience under the Covenant of Moses. If there was no obedience then not only was Israel not blessed, but she was cursed and punished by God - as Deuteronomy 28 goes on to make clear.

4b. <u>New Agreement</u>: Unconditional blessings

Under the Covenant of Christ, the Christian receives, John 1:16, *"From the fullness of His grace...one blessing after another."* Now the blessings are dependent not upon a person's efforts and a person's obedience; they are dependent solely upon God's grace.

5a. <u>Old Agreement</u>: Limited in time

The Covenant of Moses, the Old Agreement, was limited in time. It had a beginning and it had a Biblically declared end. In Galatians 3:19 Paul, writing about the Law, says, *"It was added because of transgressions UNTIL the Seed to whom the promise referred had come."* In Galatians 3:16 Paul has already explained that *"...the Seed..."* referred to is Jesus Christ. So, the Law was given to Israel and was to apply until the coming of Christ - or, more specifically, until the death of Christ.

From the moment the Law of Moses, including the Ten Commandments, was given, it had an end point. That end point was Calvary's cross because it was there that the Law was fulfilled, abolished, and cancelled - Ephesians 2:15; Colossians 2:14.

5b. <u>New Agreement</u>: Eternal

On the other hand, the Gospel of Christ is eternal. Hebrews 13:20, as one example amongst many, says as much, *"May the God of peace who, through the blood of the eternal covenant brought back from the dead our Lord Jesus..."* As it is an eternal Covenant, the Covenant of Christ was in place – albeit not revealed before Jesus - before time began, before Abraham and before the Law of Moses.

6a. <u>Old Agreement</u>: No righteousness

The word righteousness means "right standing before God" – someone in whom God finds no fault(s). Obedience to the Law of Moses cannot and was never intended to give righteousness to an individual. Romans 9:31-32, *"...Israel, who pursued a Law of righteousness has not attained it. Why not? Because they pursued it not by faith but as if it were by works."* Even though Paul could write about himself in Philippians 3:6, that *"...as for legalistic righteousness, faultless,"* he came to realise that he still fell so far short of the glory of God that he needed a Saviour. Indeed, as Paul writes in Galatians 2:21, *"...if righteousness could be gained through The Law, Christ died for nothing."*

6b. <u>New Agreement</u>: Righteousness

On the other hand, under the Covenant of Christ, Christians are given righteousness as a gift. Romans 5:17 speaks of how those *"...who receive God's abundant provision of grace and of the <u>gift</u> of righteousness* (will) *reign in life through the one man, Jesus Christ."* Righteousness, which could never be earned under the Old Covenant, is now a gift under the New Covenant. The Old Covenant had Israel struggling to achieve righteousness and utterly failing; the New Covenant leaves the Christian in receipt of the gift of righteousness, the gift of right standing before God.

Some would still teach that a Christian must contribute something towards how they stand before God. That is where so much of the struggling and disillusionment comes from in the life of a Christian - a sense of having failed God and, having fallen so short of His desired standard, become unacceptable to God. Yet the Good News of the Gospel of Christ is that a Christian cannot fall short of God's required standard for salvation because that standard is met only by Christ and the benefits of Christ's work are then freely given to the Christian.

7a. <u>Old Agreement</u>: Imprisonment

Galatians 3:23 states: *"Before this faith came, we were held prisoners by the Law, locked up until faith should be revealed."* The Law held its followers as prisoners! The limit upon this imprisonment, this Law, is set out in this same verse of Scripture: *"...we were held prisoners by the Law, locked up <u>UNTIL</u> faith should be revealed."*

7b. <u>New Agreement</u>: Freedom

In contrast, while the Law imprisoned its followers, Jesus Christ sets Christians free. Galatians 5:1, *"It is for freedom that Christ has set us free."* Christ has set Christians free from the Law; faith has been revealed. Christians must follow the instruction of Galatians 5:1, *"Stand firm, then, and do not let yourselves be burdened again by a yoke of slavery."*

8a. <u>Old Agreement</u>: Not God's will for Christians

Some would argue that "The Commandments are a good rule of life, anyway, and it doesn't do any harm to try and live by them." There is no Divine mandate for the Christian to try and live according to the Ten Commandments or any other aspects of the Law; so, to seek to obey the Law does harm because it puts that person outside of the will of God and into a partially legalistic, works-based relationship with God.

8b. <u>New Agreement</u>: God's will for Christians

Matthew 5:21 compared with Matthew 5:22 illustrates why upholding the Ten Commandments is not God's will for the Christian. In Matthew 5:21 Jesus reminds His listeners of the sixth of the Ten Commandments when He says, *"You have heard that it was said to the people long ago, do not murder and anyone who murders will be subject to judgment."* Jesus then goes on, Matthew 5:22, to reveal God's will for the Christian living under the New Agreement, *"But I tell you, that anyone who is angry with his brother will be subject to judgment."*

Those who argue in favour of the Law being applied to Christians are arguing for a lower standard of living than Jesus lays down for His people. Jesus can fairly lay down that higher standard because He gives Christians the Holy Spirit to outwork the New Agreement's standards. It isn't good enough anymore simply not to kill people. As a result of the revelation of Christ's love, and the gift of the Holy Spirit, the Christian is required not even to be angry with people. This higher standard applies to every area of a Christian's life.

9a. <u>Old Agreement</u>: Shadow

In Hebrews 10:1 it is written, *"The Law is only a shadow of the good things that are coming - not the realities themselves."*

9b. <u>New Agreement</u>: Reality

Colossians 2:17 tells where those realities are to be found, *"These* (the things of the Law) *are a shadow of the things that were to come; the reality, however, is found in Christ."* Christians should live their lives not according to a shadow but in the reality of a relationship with Jesus Christ, and all that He is and all that He has achieved.

10a. <u>Old Agreement</u>: Distant relationship

A distant relationship with God was declared by God with the giving of the Law when, in Exodus 19:24, God instructed Moses: *"Go down and bring Aaron up with you. But the priests and the people must not force their way through to come up to the Lord, or He will break out against them."* This distant relationship continued throughout the days of the Old Agreement. The High Priest was the only one who could minister before God in the Temple. When he did, it was necessary to wear bells on his priestly robes so that God would hear the bells and the High Priest would not die as he entered or left the Holy Place.

10b. <u>New Agreement</u>: Family intimacy

On the other hand, in Christ, Christians are given a spirit that cries, Romans 8:15, *"Abba, Father."* Christians are offered not distance, but intimacy, not servanthood, but sonship.

Unless Christians understand the differences between these two Covenants and can separate them and live under the one which is appropriate to them, there will always be confusion in the Christian's relationship with God. One minute the freedom of Christ - the next the imprisonment of the Law; one minute intimacy and love - the next, distance and fear. Christians in such a position have very little Good News to share with others.

A Biblical confirmation

The Bible confirms that the grace Covenant, the New Agreement, under which Christians live is not in any way affected by the Covenant of Moses. When Paul contrasts the Covenant of the Law and the Covenant of grace in Galatians 3:17 he writes, *"What I mean is this: the Law, introduced 430 years later,"* (that is, 430 years after God's covenant with Abraham) *"does not set aside the Covenant previously established by God and thus do away with the Promise."*

God established a Covenant of grace through faith with Abraham. Abraham believed God and it was credited to him as righteousness, (Genesis 15:6). Paul writes, in Gal 3:16, that, *"The promises were spoken to Abraham and to his seed."* Paul explains that the Bible does not say "and to seeds," meaning many people, but *"and to your seed,"* which refers to one person: Christ. Paul is making it clear that the heir of Abraham is not Israel, but Jesus Christ - one man. Galatians 3 explains a very important doctrinal point. The Covenant of grace through faith was with Abraham, long before the Law was given. A Covenant, the Bible says, cannot be added to or taken away from. Christ is the heir of the Abrahamic Covenant and Christians are heirs through Jesus. Accordingly, the Law has no relevance to the Christians as they are under another, earlier, Covenant. Gal 3:29 says, *"If you belong to Christ, then you are Abraham's seed and heirs according to The Promise."*

So there is the Biblical confirmation that Christians are utterly unaffected by the Law of Moses, and should not be living under it, not applying it to their relationship with God nor teaching it to others as a relevant rule of life or moral code.

Christ's two Covenant ministry

As we continue to look at separating the Old and New Covenants, it is important to realise that Jesus Christ had a two-Covenant ministry. He was, as Simeon declared in Luke 1:32, both, *"...a light for revelation to the Gentiles and for glory to Your people Israel."* Jesus Christ was the long-awaited Prophet for Israel, but He was also the one to proclaim salvation to the Gentiles (Isaiah 42:6). Jesus came to end one Covenant and, then, started a New Covenant.

Failure to recognise these two Covenant ministries leads to utter confusion when looking at the teachings of Christ. When speaking to Israel,

Jesus spoke as someone living under the Law of Moses. He had to do this because Israel, and Jesus as an Israelite, was under the Law of Moses and, as Jesus said in Matthew 5:18, the Law would remain in place, "*...until everything is accomplished.*" That is why Jesus, when answering the lawyer in Luke 10, pointed out obedience to the Law as the way to inherit eternal life (Lk 10:25-28).

When speaking in His role as Messiah, Jesus spoke as the initiator of the New Covenant. Thus, in John 6:28-29, when others came and asked, "*What must we do to do the works God requires?*" Jesus does not point them to the Law but, to Himself when He replies, "*The work of God is this: to believe in the One He has sent.*"

Those two teachings of Jesus are irreconcilable. In one Jesus says that obedience to the Law of Moses is the way to be right with God, in the other Jesus says that faith in Him is the way to get right with God. There are many such instances in the teachings of Christ, where one teaching appears to contradict another. They actually do contradict each other - because the two Covenants contradict each other. Grace is not Law, faith is not works, eternal is not limited and so on. In another sense, though, the teachings of Jesus are never contradictory; it is simply that the New Covenant is replacing the Old. That replacement did not fully take place until, at Calvary's cross, "*...everything is accomplished,*" hence the need for the dual approach adopted by Jesus - one for the Jews and one for the whole world, including the Jews.

Jesus, as a Jew born under the Law, and living under the Law, could not speak against the Law - it was the God-given rule of life for the Jew. Jesus, as the Son of God and Saviour of both Jew and Gentile, could not uphold the Law but must rather uphold grace. Unless Christians are aware of, and accept this two-Covenant ministry, they will be left with countless Scriptures which are impossible to reconcile.

The real problem arises when Christians, unaware of Christ's two-fold ministry, read Luke 10:25-28. In this passage, Jesus tells the lawyer that obedience to the Law is the way to inherit eternal life. Many may mistakenly believe that this applies to them as Christians as well.

An important question to ask whenever reading the teachings of Jesus is, "Who was He speaking to? In what role was He giving this teaching?"

Without such questioning, there is no distinction between Jesus' teachings as someone living under the Law and the One who came to fulfil and abolish the Law. (Ephesians 2:15, Colossians 2:14).

Understanding this two-Covenant ministry removes any confusion from what Jesus taught. It becomes apparent that, when speaking as Messiah of the world, Jesus excluded the Law from all His teaching.

The Apostle Paul's move from Moses to Christ

Paul - The Jew

Paul, before his conversion, was a zealous follower of the Law of Moses. He writes of himself, in Philippians 3:5-6, "...*circumcised on the eighth day, of the people of Israel, of the tribe of Benjamin, a Hebrew of Hebrews; in regard to the Law, a Pharisee; as for zeal, persecuting the church; as for legalistic righteousness, faultless.*"

Paul - The Christian

How dramatically Paul turned his back on that position can be seen from his writing in 1 Cor 9:20-22. The man who had described himself as "...*a Hebrew of Hebrews*" now writes, "*To the Jews I became as a Jew...*" As a Christian, **Paul no longer thinks of himself as a Jew**. He no longer lives as a Jew. As someone who no longer saw himself as a Jew, Paul was no longer bound by the Law because that only applied to the Jews. Much of Paul's troubles, reflected in his writings, came because he was often accused of setting aside the Law of Moses and teaching others to do the same. Here Paul writes that he reverted to his Jewish position only to win fellow Jews to Christ.

Paul then makes his position very clear, and therefore every Christian's position very clear regarding the Law. He writes, "*To those under the Law I became like one under the Law (though* **I myself am not under the Law)**...*"*Paul boldly proclaims that he is not under the Law. Christians who seek to, or teach others to, live under the Law - even if it is only the Ten Commandments as a rule of life - are taking a position contrary to the life and teachings of the Apostle Paul. If the Law did not apply to Paul it cannot apply to any Christian.

In his next utterance, Paul answers those who say that to fully embrace the grace in the New Covenant will lead to license. Paul writes, "*To those not having the Law*" (that is the Gentiles) "*I became like one not having the Law (though* **I am not free from God's law but am under Christ's law).**" This is the first reference in the New Testament to the law which replaced the Law of Moses. It is the first reference to the rule of life which applies to Christians.

Hebrews 7:12, *"For when the priesthood is changed, the law must be changed also."* During the time of Moses, Aaron, Moses' brother, was appointed as the High Priest of Israel. On Aaron's death, the High Priesthood of Israel passed down through Aaron's direct descendants. At the time of Christ, the Law of Moses was still in force and Aaron's descendants were still the High Priests of Israel.

When Jesus came, died and rose again He became the new High Priest. Hebrews 4:14 says, *"Therefore since we have a great high priest who has ascended into heaven, Jesus the Son of God, let us hold firmly to the faith we profess."* The Bible teaches that the priesthood changed from Aaron's descendants to Jesus; so, the Law (of Moses) also had to change - as Paul confirms it did, to the law of Christ.

Finally, it is worth noting that Paul finishes this passage by saying, *"To the weak, I became weak..."* Living under Christ's law, living under grace, was a source of strength to Paul and he only left that position and *"became weak"* in order *"to win the weak"* – that is, those living under the Old Agreement.

Some New Testament Scriptures on the Law

Understanding what the New Testament teaches about the Law (the Old Agreement) will stop the tendency which exists today of placing Christians under aspects of the Law. This is a look at just a few of the many New Testament Scriptures which deal with the Law and its relationship to the Christian.

Love - not legalism. Matthew 12:1-8 In this passage, Jesus and His disciples are walking through a cornfield on the Sabbath, and His disciples begin to pick some of the corn to eat. The Pharisees immediately question Jesus about why He is allowing His disciples to break the Law – the Law forbids any work on the Sabbath, even collecting food. Jesus' answer includes the statement, *"If you had known what these words mean, 'I desire mercy, not sacrifice,' you would not have condemned the innocent."* Jesus is pointing the Pharisees beyond the legalism of Moses and towards the Law of Love (the law of Christ). The disciples' actions in this passage violated the Fourth Commandment. Jesus is showing that in Him the Law of Moses is fulfilled and abolished. Love now takes pre-eminence.

Christians not under The Law. Acts 15:5-11 In this passage, the significance of the Law for Christians is clarified, and a consensus is reached by the Apostles. Some Jews who had become Christians had been teaching new Gentile Christians that unless they were circumcised, that is, put themselves under the authority of the Law, they could not be saved. After much discussion amongst the Apostles and elders, Peter addresses the early Christians. In his address, he asks the question, of those who would apply the Law to the new Christians, *"Now then, why do you test God by putting on the necks of the disciples a yoke that neither we nor our fathers have been able to bear? No! We believe it is through the grace of our Lord Jesus that we are saved, just as they are."* Anyone, today, seeking to put a Christian under any aspect of the Law, usually in the form of the Ten Commandments or a more general legalistic obedience, should be asked the same question, "Why are you doing that?"

No Law - no sin. Romans 7:8 This Scripture gives a very strong and clear reason why Christians should resist any attempt to put them under the Law. This verse says, in part, *"For apart from Law, sin is dead."* That is part of the Good News of the New Covenant. Those struggling with sin today do not need to strive or make superhuman efforts to free themselves from it. Such a struggling Christian must simply come out from under the law and live in grace. Romans 5:17 says that *"...those who receive God's abundant provision of grace and of the gift of righteousness* (will) *reign in life through the one man, Jesus Christ."* What hope, what peace, and what joy can be offered to the struggling Christians when they are pointed not to themselves but to the cross of Christ! Romans 4:15 makes the same point: *"And where there is no Law there is no transgression."* John 3:4 says, *"Everyone who sins breaks the Law..."* Clearly, if the Law is removed so, is sin. And that is the achievement of Christ on Calvary's cross. The Law was removed and so was sin. Many Christians still believe that sin is an issue between the Christian and God, but the Good News is that both the Law and sin have been dealt with by Jesus.

The Law gives sin its power. I Corinthians 15:56 For those struggling with sin it is encouraging to know that it is the Law which gives sin its power - for that is what this Scripture says. Anyone battling to overcome sin must, therefore, set aside the legalism which so defeats and demoralises, and live in the grace which God extends to humanity through Jesus in the New Covenant. The Law does not have the power to force a person to repeat old habits or thought patterns; rather, its power lies in instilling feelings of guilt, failure, and condemnation. This can lead a Christian to withdraw from fellowship with God and other believers. Just as the Law, when originally given to Moses, initiated a distant relationship with the Lord, so the Law today brings that same distancing. The Law has the power to isolate and weaken even further. That is the power the Law gives to sin. Accordingly, any attempt to impose any aspects of the Law on a Christian should be resisted.

The Law abolished. Ephesians 2:14-15 This Scripture states that Jesus Christ abolished the Law. All major translations of The Bible use the word "*abolished*" or "*abolishing*" regarding what Christ has done to the Law. So even those who find it difficult to accept that the Ten Commandments (and the rest of the Law) <u>never</u> applied to the Christian must accept that the Law no longer applies. Christians should always point others to Jesus and His achievement; not to an obsolete "Jewish Law" - as the Good News translation refers to it. Colossians 2:14 speaks of God "...*having cancelled the written code...*" Some argue that this refers only to the ceremonial law but Colossians 2:16 makes specific reference to the fourth Commandment, the keeping of the Sabbath. The Law, in its entirety, has been cancelled because of the New Agreement.

Obey all The Law - or none. James 2:10 The Christian Church has made a "sacred cow" out of the Ten Commandments and chosen to ignore most of the rest of the Law of Moses. Yet James writes here that if anyone seeks to keep the Law then such a person must keep ALL the Law. If a person breaks one point of the Law, James states that they have effectively broken all of the Law. Some may argue that only the Ten Commandments were given directly by God, while the others were added by man. However, the early books of the Bible contain many rules and regulations that are included in Scripture and 2 Timothy 3:16 which states that "*All Scripture is God breathed....*" So, Christians cannot ignore hundreds of Scriptural rules and commands and simply seek to hold on to the Ten Commandments; there is no integrity in such a position or such a teaching.

These Scripture verses are but a handful of many similar verses throughout the New Testament in the Bible. All such verses prove beyond doubt that the Law of Moses was given for a limited period of time, for a specific purpose and only to a specific group of people. All Christians – that is all who believe in Jesus, whether Messianic Jews or Gentiles, now live under Christ's law, a law of love.

The Commandments of Christ

One of the objections of those who oppose grace in all its fullness is the fact that Jesus gave commandments and, they argue, these HAVE to be obeyed - even if the Law of Moses doesn't.

Jesus did, indeed, give many commandments to His followers; however, Jesus did not use the phrase, *"My commandment"* until the last supper. The reason for this is that at the last supper, the whole of His talk to the disciples is set after the cross. That whole section of Scripture, John 13 to John 17, is Jesus speaking as the Saviour of the world. He is speaking as One who has ended the rule of the Law of Moses. If the Law were still applicable, He would have neither the need nor the right to impose new commandments. All the commandments, therefore, of Christ are given within the grace dispensation. In the passage of Scripture John 13 to John 17 there is only one reference to the Law of Moses. It is in John 15:25. Speaking of the events that are to unfold after the last supper, Jesus says, *"But this is to fulfil what is written in **their** Law: 'They hated Me without reason.'"* In this one reference to the Law of Moses, Jesus is clearly disassociating Himself and, thereby, His followers from the Law of the Jews.

The commandments given by Christ form what Paul refers to as *"Christ's law"* (1 Cor 9:21). They are given to be obeyed; however, it must be remembered that they are given, and only take effect, within the Covenant of grace. These commandments given by Jesus represent the only Biblical 'Rule of Life' for the Christian. Any other rule of life, including adherence to the Old Covenant in any way, is self-imposed and has no biblical mandate or Divine authority behind it.

The nature of Christ's commandments makes clear that they do, indeed, come under the New Covenant. The New Covenant, the new law, is a Covenant, a law, of grace and love. Many of Christ's teachings and actions demonstrate the supremacy of love over legalism. It was this issue that brought Him into such direct conflict with the Pharisees and teachers of the Law. Christ's commandments reflect this supremacy of love. In His teaching at the Last Supper, Jesus instructs His followers, *"A new command I give you: love* one another. *As I have loved you, so you must love one another.*" In John 15:12 Jesus says, "*My command is this: love each other as I have loved you.*" Again, in John 15:17, Jesus says, "*This is My command: Love each other.*" In 2 John verse 6 the apostle writes, "*As you have heard from the beginning, His command is that you walk in love.*" The Apostle Paul sums up the commands of Christ when writing to the Galatians. In his letter, Paul writes in Gal 6:2, "*Carry each other's burdens, and in this way, you will fulfil the law of Christ.*"

So there are commandments for Christians to obey. Setting aside the Law of Moses does not leave the Christian living a lawless, licentious life. The commands given by Christ, however, are set within the grace Covenant so whether the Christian obeys them or not will not affect their standing before God. Ignoring the commands of Christ will have a detrimental effect on the Christian's witness and the well-being of others, and that is the motivation for keeping Christ's commands. It is not fear of punishment, and not fear of being loved less or blessed less by God - it is love of God and others that motivates a Christian to live as Christ commands. This is the mark of the Christian, as Christ Himself said in John 13:35, "*By this all men will know you are My disciples, if you love one another.*"

Conclusion

The Old Covenant, based not on spiritual gifts from God but on an individual's obedience to hundreds of divinely given laws, was never intended for, nor biblically applicable to, non-Jews. Accordingly, not applying the Old Covenant to their life means that, far from abandoning or rejecting a part of the Bible, the Christian is living in full accord with Biblical teachings and God's will for the Christian's life. That is the resolution of the supposed dilemma with which the Church, and individual Christians, have struggled for centuries.

The foundational doctrine of the New Agreement is that: A person is saved through two acts of grace from God towards that individual. Firstly, the gift of God's Son, Jesus Christ, to be the bearer of God's punishment due to all humanity for every sin ever committed and, secondly, the gift of faith to believe that truth.

Receiving those two divine gifts is all that is required for salvation – which is an uninterrupted, eternal relationship with God, through Jesus, from the moment of first believing in Jesus in this life, and on throughout eternity following the Christian's departure from this life into the next.

With this understanding, the individual Christian, and the Church generally, will experience a return of Biblical Christianity – lived out through the power of the Holy Spirit and impacting others in a way that the confusion of the all-to-prevalent "blending" of the Agreements hinders and prevents. Biblically-based Christians, living in God's grace free from the Law will then again see the Gospel *"...bearing fruit and growing throughout the whole world..."* (Colossians 1:6).

Chapter 2

The doctrine of grace

Modern Teaching

Grace is the doctrine that is the heart of the Gospel. Modern teaching, the "blending" of Old and New Covenants, teaches that Christians are saved by grace, but that Christians shouldn't take grace "too far." Modern Christianity teaches that Christians should, while understanding they are saved by grace through faith, make every effort to maintain their ongoing salvation and not risk slipping into a licentious way of life by abusing grace.

According to the modern teaching of Christianity, a Christian's salvation depends upon God's grace and the Christian's efforts to live the Christian life. Striving against sin and striving to be a better Christian is taught as the way of life for a Christian.

Incorporating a Christian's lifestyle into their ongoing relationship with God, and even considering it a factor in their salvation, diminishes the joy of their salvation. This approach undermines the certainty and assurance that should accompany their salvation. The absence of joy and spiritual insecurity can weaken a Christian's ability to share God's grace effectively. As a result, the message of the Good News can become a confusing mix of positive and negative aspects. It conveys the idea: "You are saved, but now you need to ensure you hold onto that!"

What follows is the Bible's teachings on New Covenant grace which, when properly understood, restores the joy of their salvation to Christians, reveals the source of their eternal spiritual security and helps deepen their relationship with God– who accepts them totally, just the way they are – and it's all Good News!

Part 1:
Understanding grace

Introduction

Ephesians 1:4-6

"For He chose us in Him before the creation of the world to be holy and blameless in His sight. In love, He predestined us for adoption to sonship through Jesus Christ, in accordance with His pleasure and will - to the praise of His glorious grace, which He has freely given us in the One He loves."

The foundational truth of grace

The one foundational truth about grace, as Ephesians 1:4-6 makes abundantly clear, is that grace is freely and undeservedly given. It is from this truth that all other truths about grace flow. It is this one foundational truth which assures the Christians of their security in their salvation. As grace is freely and undeservedly given, it is given without regard to what is going on in the recipient's life, either at the time grace is extended or thereafter. This means that **grace is given** to the recipient:

(i) Without regard to lifestyle. A person becomes a Christian by accepting that they are a lost sinner and by trusting in Jesus Christ for their salvation. That trust is based on the truth that when Jesus died on Calvary's cross, He was being punished for every sin the Christian had committed or ever would commit. Thus, God maintains His perfect justice, and His hatred of sin, and yet can be gracious towards the sinner. This situation is maintained after the point of conversion. In other words, although the Christian will certainly go on failing to live up to God's requirement of holiness, God will continue to extend His grace and blessings to that person - including the gracious blessing (and gift) of eternal life - because the sacrifice of Jesus has already paid for the sins committed before and after conversion.

There is only one answer to sin and that is the blood of Christ shed on the cross. That answer applies to all sins for all people for all time. 1 John 2:2, makes it clear that sins of lifestyle are no longer an issue between God and humanity: *"He is the atoning sacrifice for our sins, and not only for ours but also for the sins of the whole world."* The only issue now between God and humanity, the Scriptures make clear, is belief in or rejection of Jesus as the Son of God. John 3:18 says that a person stands condemned, *"...because he has not believed in the name of God's one and only Son."*

The issue between God and humanity is not the details of how a person lives their individual, daily life; but what that person believes about Jesus. That is why, without compromising His divine justice, God can still regard a Christian who constantly fails to meet God's requirement of holiness as His saved child. A Christian is saved, and remains saved because of faith in Christ's achievement on their behalf, not by works. Thus, the fundamental principle of grace is that it is offered freely and without merit. This means that a Christian's lifestyle does not influence their standing before God, neither in this life nor in the afterlife. Any teaching that instils insecurity and fear into a Christian about their standing before God, is rooted in a works-centred salvation and, as such, stands opposed to the cross of Christ and should be resolutely resisted.

(ii) Without regard to the response. Grace, in order to truly be grace, must be given freely. This means that God extends it to all without strings or conditions. The Scriptures always refer to eternal life as a gift, which must be free. The truth, therefore, must be that if the gift of eternal life is to remain a gift, then it must be given without regard to the response of the recipient. The astonishing reality is that God's gift of His Son Jesus, and all that flows through Him, puts the Christian under no obligation whatsoever. This lack of obligation must include the lack of obligation to live in a certain way or according to a certain standard.

The lifestyle of a Christian after salvation is often seen as a threat to their eternal security and salvation. However, the truth is that a person's way of life, whether before or after their conversion, has no impact on their standing before God and, consequently, their security in salvation. If a Christian accepts any obligation because of the gift of salvation - the commonest being that the Christian should strive against sin and seek to improve their way of life - then that Christian puts God, effectively, in the supposed position of saying, "I give you eternal life as a gift; but in order to keep that gift you are required to...." Such is the substance of so much wrong teaching today.

Christians are often told that God's attitude toward them, including their eternal salvation, fluctuates based on their daily lifestyle and efforts. This teaching contradicts a wealth of Scripture. Those who teach such error do so because they have not understood the empowerment that comes through grace, and wrongly see grace, fully embraced, as a road to license. Thus, the core truth about grace is that it is given freely and without deserving. This means that a Christian's response after salvation does not affect their standing before God, either in this life or in the life to come. Any teaching to the contrary tarnishes the great gift of Jesus, reduces that gift to a mere exchange and should be, again, resolutely resisted.

What is grace?

God's Riches At Christ's Expense is a simple expression to explain grace. The Christian has laid before them the riches of God - *"...every spiritual blessing in Christ"* (Ephesians 1:3). That which is Christ's is also the Christian's.

"And God raised us up with Christ and seated us with Him in the heavenly realms in Christ Jesus" (Ephesians 2:6). That which God has, by His grace, chosen to bestow on every Christian is not free. There is an enormous price tag attached to the exalted position occupied by the Christian. The Good News of the Gospel is that Jesus Christ has paid the price - in full. As Jesus bore the punishment due to every person because of their sins, God the Father is now free to pour out the unlimited love and blessings that He has for every Christian.

Five reasons to fully understand grace

1. There is an understanding amongst some that grace is an easy option, even an alternative to obedience, yet the Bible reveals the very opposite. Romans 5:1-2 says, *"Therefore since we have been justified through faith, we have peace with God through our Lord Jesus Christ, through whom we have gained access by faith into this grace in which we now stand."* It is grace that enables the Christian to stand. 1 Peter 5:12 makes the same point when Peter writes about what he terms, *"...the true grace of God"* and then urges his readers to, *"Stand fast in it."* Repeatedly it will be seen in the Bible that grace is the source of power and Christian living for the Christian, and it is for that reason that the truth of grace must be grasped.

2. Romans 5:17 is a verse of great promise on the power of grace to transform the life of a Christian. It says, *"...how much more will those who receive God's abundant provision of grace and of the gift of righteousness reign in life through the one man, Jesus Christ."* Here is a two-fold promise: firstly, that God's grace is provided in abundance and secondly, that whoever receives this abundant grace will reign in life. Not understanding the grace revealed in the New Covenant means missing out on this two-fold promise. So, for this reason, the truth of grace must be understood.

3. The Christian who receives grace will work harder for the Kingdom than the Christian who strives in their own strength. The Apostle Paul, a renowned worker for the Kingdom of God, writes in 1 Corinthians 15:10, *"But by the grace of God I am what I am, and His grace to me was not without effect. No, I worked harder than all of them - yet not I, but the grace of God that was with me."* Paul's testimony is that receiving grace produces much hard work for the Kingdom. Not understanding God's grace reduces the effectiveness of the individual Christian and the Church as a whole. So, for this reason, God's grace must be understood.

4. For those sufficiently caught up in their sin that they despair of ever being free of sinful ways, habits or thoughts, the Bible points to grace as the way of overcoming sin. The promise to the Christian, in Romans 6:14, is, *"Sin shall not be your master, because you are not under law, but under grace."* Not living fully under the grace of the New Covenant results in a heightened awareness by the Christians of their supposed sins, shortcomings and failings and, as a result, Christianity can become for many a constant struggle to be a "better" Christian – thus reducing that Christians' outreach and service of the Gospel to a minimum. For this reason, God's grace must be understood, grasped and lived in.

5. Colossians 1:6 declares the absolute necessity of understanding grace to bear fruit and grow. It says, *"All over the world this gospel is* *bearing fruit and growing, just as it has been doing among you <u>since</u> the day you heard it and understood God's grace in all its truth.*" It is the <u>understanding</u> of grace that produces growth and fruit, so for this reason God's grace must be properly understood and fully grasped.

The reasons listed here, and others revealed in the Bible, make it clear that Biblical Christianity – receiving God's grace and living fully in the New Covenant – releases the Christian into a powerful, purpose-filled new way of living. A new way of living that enables the Christian to stand strong, overcome the trials and tribulations of life, work hard for the Gospel, overcome personal un-Christian ways and bear fruit for the Kingdom of God.

Some truths about grace

1. God's grace is not dependent upon, nor connected to, any human effort or lack of effort by either a Christian or a non-Christian. God's grace is independent of any pressures, considerations or any other factors that may be thought to lessen or increase the grace extended by God to the recipient. The extending of God's grace, whether to humanity as a whole or to an individual, is solely God's sovereign choice and cannot be influenced by external factors.

One Bible verse that proves the bestowing of God's grace is unconnected to any human effort or input is 2 Timothy 1:9 which tells us when God's grace was extended to humanity: *"This grace was given to us in Christ Jesus before the beginning of time"* Before time began or humanity existed, God chose to be gracious to humanity and send His Son, Jesus, as the Saviour of all who will believe.

2. The bestowing of God's grace is not affected by sin. Some may believe that God is withholding His grace from them for a period because of sin in their lives, but such a belief ignores the most basic truth of the Christian Gospel - that ALL sin was taken away and placed upon Christ at Calvary's cross.

That nothing and no-one affects God's decision to bestow His grace is borne out in Romans 5:8, *"God demonstrates His own love for us in this: While we were still sinners Christ died for us."* God is gracious regardless of how any individual is living and the gift of Christ, given *"...while we were still sinners,"* is the ultimate proof.

3. Grace is not lessened because of the way an individual is living. Just as grace is not completely withheld from an individual, so grace cannot be given in a reduced or partial manner. Jesus Christ came, John 1:14, *"FULL of grace and truth."* John 1:16 says that it was *"From the FULLNESS of His grace...."* God is not able to be partially gracious. It is in the very character of God to be gracious, and He will, and indeed must, always be true to Himself. If a Christian's lifestyle determines the extent to which God bestows His grace upon that Christian, it would mean that grace is something which must be earned - which, in turn, would mean that it is not grace at all.

4. Grace carries NO strings. Ephesians 1:6 testifies to the truth of the nature of grace when it says, *"...to the praise of His glorious grace, which He has **freely** given us in the One He loves."* The stark truth is that despite the enormity of God's gift to humanity in the form of His Son Jesus, humanity – collectively and individually - is under no obligation whatsoever to God because of that gift. If the gift carries any obligation, then it is no longer a gift. This is good news because as Christians are not under any obligation, then they cannot fail God or let God down.

All that God, through Jesus Christ, has achieved for humanity is described as a gift - eternal life (John 10:28, Romans 6:23), the Holy Spirit (Acts 1:4, Acts 2:38), repentance and forgiveness of sins (Acts 5:31), righteousness (Romans 5:17) and so on. As with any gift, God's grace comes without any thought of the recipient becoming obligated in some way to the gift-giver. This truth is Good News for the Christian because it removes any need for striving to pay God back, to be more worthy of His grace, or to show gratitude for the grace extended. It is free and unconditional.

5. *God's forgiveness of the sins of a Christian is an outworking of His justice, not His grace.* The sending of the substitute Lamb of God, Jesus, to bear the punishment for sin was God's act of grace. God does not punish the Christians for their sin because the penalty has already been borne by Jesus. Therefore, there is no outstanding punishment due to the Christian. It is a simple matter of Divine justice.

God's grace as revealed by Jesus

Mark 2:1-12 _Healing the paralytic_. In response to the faith of the paralytic and his friends, Jesus forgives the paralytic his sins and then physically heals him. Jesus makes no demands, and sets no conditions - He sees a need, sees their faith and graciously responds.

Luke 15:20-24: _The welcoming of the lost son_. The welcome extended to the lost son began even when the son was _"…still a long way off."_ The father made no demands of the son, made no enquiries about how he had spent the money, whether was there any left, how it would be paid back and so on. The father set down no conditions such as the son needing to work to pay back the loss. The father's one intention was to offer to restore a broken relationship, and to himself bear the cost brought about through the son's actions. In this passage is a powerful illustration of God's attitude to humanity. God is willing to bear the cost of humanity's sins and to graciously restore the saved sinner to a position as a son within God's household.

Luke 19:1-10 _Zacchaeus_. When Jesus announced to Zacchaeus, _"I must stay at your house today."_ He put no conditions upon His gracious offer to stay under the roof of a tax collector. He did not demand that Zacchaeus stop being a tax collector. He did not demand that Zacchaeus pay back anyone he had cheated. The fact is that, as he received Jesus' grace Zacchaeus became a changed man and voluntarily repaid those he had cheated. This is Good News for the Christian as the message here is that receiving grace brings about change, not striving to be "better."

John 21:15-19: _Jesus re-instates Peter_. After he denied Jesus, during the time surrounding Jesus' trial, Peter _"…went outside and wept bitterly"_ (Lk 22:62). Jesus had already declared that whoever denied Him before men would be denied by Jesus before the Father in heaven (Matt 10:32). With this background, with Peter's demonstrated awareness of how he had betrayed Jesus, their meeting on the beach, in this passage in John, could have been entirely different. Instead, it gives a wonderful illustration of how Jesus graciously restored His zealous, but very human, follower. What Good News for every Christian whose heart cries "Yes, Lord," but whose flesh leads them down a contrary path. This encounter once again shows Jesus making no demands of Peter, no promises extracted regarding any further denials, no reprimand issued - just a gracious, freely offered reinstatement.

Conclusion

The need to fully understand grace, the foundational truths about grace, and the greatest illustration of God's grace in action are all very clearly expressed in two Bible verses: Colossians 1:21-22, *"Once you were alienated from God and were enemies in your minds because of your evil behaviour. But now He has reconciled you by Christ's physical body through death to present you holy in His sight, without blemish and free from accusation..."*

Part 2:
Secure in grace

The following Bible teachings illustrate how a Christian is completely secure in their salvation by showing that a Christian's security in their salvation is entirely a work of God for humanity.

God's purposes for the Christian

There are in the Scriptures two identifiable purposes behind God's grace towards the Christian, and both these purposes ensure the Christian's safe-keeping in grace.

The two purposes are:

(a) The _future_ displaying of God's grace.

Ephesians 2:6-7- *"And God raised us up with Christ and seated us with Him in the heavenly realms in order that **in the coming ages** He might show the incomparable riches of His grace, expressed in His kindness to us in Christ Jesus."* This Scripture shows that one purpose behind God's grace towards the Christian will not be fulfilled until *"...the coming ages."*

There are two things to consider about this Scripture regarding a Christian's security in salvation. Firstly, if a Christian contributes anything at all towards their being *"...raised up and seated with Christ..."* then God will not be able to display that Christian as a trophy of pure grace. Yet it is God's intention, in a time still to come, to show through the Christians in heaven, the breadth and depth of His amazing grace. The Christian, therefore, remains secure in their salvation because of grace and God's purpose in that grace.

The second thing to say about this Scripture is that God's purpose in grace is not fulfilled when the Christian becomes saved. God's purpose will not be fulfilled until *"…the coming ages."* If a Christian's safe-keeping in salvation depended, in any way, upon the Christian's contribution then God could have no guarantee that He would be left with any trophies of grace to display. For the Christians to be the witness *"…in the coming ages…"* to God's grace then the Christians must be saved by grace and must be kept secure in salvation by that same grace. God's purpose will be fulfilled only because God is the guarantor.

(b) The outworking of <u>*pre-determined*</u> good works.

Ephesians 2:10: *"For we are God's workmanship created in Christ Jesus to do good works which God prepared <u>in advance</u> for us to do."* If the Christian's standing in the faith, or the continuance of their right relationship with God, depends in any way upon the Christian's contribution or effort then God could have no confidence that the works He prepared in advance for the Christian to do would be completed. If any of these works, pre-determined by God, is not completed then that would entirely discredit the Bible which states in Job 42:2, when speaking of God that, *"…no plan of Yours can be thwarted."* God Himself says, in Isaiah 14:24, *"Surely, as I have planned, so it will be, and as I have purposed, so it will stand."* God could safely prepare good works in advance for the Christian because He knows that it is He who will both save the Christian and, thereafter, keep the Christian saved and that, therefore, the Christian will be enabled to complete those pre-determined tasks.

God can only have long term purposes in grace, as the two outlined here, if He, and He alone, is the guarantor that those purposes will be fulfilled. The promise of 1 Corinthians 1:8 says just that, *"He* (God) *will keep you strong to the end…"*

God's gracious provision for the Christian

The Scriptures show the many provisions God has made for the Christian so that, having been saved by grace, they may remain safe and secure in their salvation through His same grace. The many provisions which God has made for the Christian all involve the Person of God in the different roles of the Holy Trinity - Father, Son and Holy Spirit, so God is wholly engaged in saving and keeping the Christian.

1. God the Father - His power

Jesus says, John 10:29, *"My Father who has given them* (the Christians) *to Me is greater than all; no one can snatch them out of My Father's hand."* The power of God guarantees the Christian's security. No one, no power, can snatch the Christian from the position they occupy in the Father's hand. Paul expresses his confidence in the keeping power of God when, in 2 Timothy 1:12, he writes, *"...I know whom I have believed, and am convinced that He is able to guard what I have entrusted to Him for that day."* Paul's confidence is in God's ability to maintain Paul's position - not in Paul's ability to maintain his own position. The Christian is kept perfectly safe by the power of God and Jude acknowledges this in verse 24 of his letter when he writes, *"To Him who is able to keep you from falling and to present you before His glorious presence without fault and with great joy..."* It is God who keeps the Christian from falling. Such understanding from the Bible of God's role in the Christian's security brings great peace to every Christian.

2. God the Father - His love

Romans 8:39; *"...nor anything else in all creation will be able to separate us* (the Christians) *from the love of God that is in Christ Jesus."* No power in the universe can separate the Christian from the love which God has for them. As nothing can separate the Christian from the love of God that includes the things that Christians fear will bring about that separation - and the most common of these is usually the lifestyle of the Christian after salvation. Romans 5:8, *"...God demonstrated His own love for us in this: while we were still sinners, Christ died for us."* It was while the Christian was still caught up in sin that God sent His Son - such is the power of His love. A love that saves, a love that secures.

3. Christ - His prayer

At the last supper Jesus prayed for His disciples and in, John 17:20, He prayed, *"My prayer is not for them* (the disciples) *alone. I pray also for those who will believe in Me* (Christians) *through their message."* Jesus declared the content of His prayer in verse 15, *"My prayer is not that You* (the Father) *take them out of the world but that You protect them from the evil one."* God the Son asked God the Father to protect the Christian from the evil one. Every Christian should be secure that having been saved, they will remain safe in their salvation - because God the Father will very obviously grant the prayer of God the Son.

Niall Walshe

4. Christ - His blood

Hebrews 9:22: *"...without the shedding of blood there is no forgiveness."* There are many Scriptures in the New Testament that tell of what Christ has achieved for humanity through the shedding of His blood. Hebrews 13:12 says; *"...Jesus also suffered outside the city gate to make the people holy through His own blood."* It is the blood of Jesus that secures holiness for the Christian. The blood has been shed and the holiness secured. Christians should rest in Christ's achievement.

5. Christ - His death

Romans 8:3 says that when Jesus Christ died, God, *"...condemned sin in sinful man."* As Paul wrote regarding sin, in Rom 7:17, *"...it is no longer I myself who do it but it is sin living in me...."* Sin is condemned, not the Christian. John 3:18 clarifies that rejection of Jesus is the only reason left for condemnation, *"Whoever believes in Him is not condemned, but whoever does not believe stands condemned already because they have not believed in the name of God's one and only Son."*

Jesus' death provides the truth of the Scripture, Romans 8:1: *"Therefore, there is now no condemnation for those who are in Christ Jesus."*

6. Christ - His resurrection

Romans 6:3-4 explains that the Christian has, through faith, shared with Christ in His death and burial. Romans 6:5 goes on to say, *"For if we have been united with Him in a death like His, we will certainly also be united with Him in a resurrection like His."* The resurrected life of Jesus Christ is within every Christian - that guarantees the spiritual safety and security of the Christian.

7. Christ - His intercession

1 John 2:1 says, *"My dear children, I write this to you so that you will not sin. But if anybody does sin, we have One who speaks to the Father in our defence - Jesus Christ, the Righteous One."* It is not the job of the Christian to plead their case before the Father. God demands a death penalty for every sin (Romans 6:23). Jesus Christ, as the One who died for all the sins ever committed or yet to be committed, is the only One qualified to speak for sinners.

Romans 8:34 says, *"Who then is the one who condemns? No one. Christ Jesus who died - more than that, who was raised to life - is at the right hand of God and is also interceding for us."* Jesus continues to demonstrate His grace towards the Christian by continually interceding for the Christian so that no one and nothing can condemn the Christian.

8. Christ - His shepherd-hood

In John 10:11 Jesus says, *"I am the good shepherd"*. The good shepherd does not wait until his flock is attacked and then seeks to defend his sheep. The good shepherd protects his flock by preventing the attack. Jesus Christ illustrates this care in Luke 22:31-32 when He informs Peter, who is unaware of the danger, *"Simon, Simon, Satan has asked to sift you as wheat. But I have prayed for you, Simon, that your faith may not fail..."* Jesus Christ knows what Satan is up to and Jesus is eternally guarding and protecting His people against the schemes of the enemy. Peter confirms this eternal shepherding ministry of Christ when he writes of Jesus, in 1 Peter 2:25, *"For you were like sheep going astray, but now you have returned to the Shepherd and Overseer of your souls."* The spiritually secure position of the Christian depends upon Jesus and not upon the Christian.

9. The Spirit - Bringing new birth

John 1:12-13 says, *"Yet to all who received Him, to those who believed in His name, He gave the right to become children of God - children born not of natural descent, nor of human decision or a husband's will, but born of God."* These are important truths which establish the secure, unalterable position of the Christian. It is *"...to those who believed"* that God gave *"the right"* to be called His children. All Christians are born of the Spirit (John 3:6). A Christian is a child of God because that is their *"...right..."* God Himself secured that right by giving Christians the faith which enabled their spiritual birth. Christians are spiritually secure because of this provision by God for their security.

10. The Spirit - Ensuring new life

The Bible says that the Spirit of God lives within every Christian. In John 7:39, it explains that the *"...rivers of living water..."* referred to by Jesus in the previous verse is *"...the Spirit, whom those who believed in Him were later to receive."* In John 14:16, Jesus says He will ask the Father to give *"...another Counsellor to be with you* (the Christians) *forever - the Spirit of Truth."* Romans 5:5 speaks of God's love being poured out into the Christian's heart *"...by the Holy Spirit, whom He has given us."* Jesus asked that the indwelling Spirit be with the Christian *"...forever..."* The Holy Spirit safeguards the Christian, for who can stand against God.

11. The Spirit - "sealing" the Christian

The Bible says that every Christian is sealed with the Holy Spirit. In 2 Corinthians 1:22, it says: God has put His seal of ownership on the Christian and *"...put His Spirit in our hearts as a deposit, guaranteeing what is to come."* It is the Holy Spirit of God who is the guarantor of the Christian's eternal inheritance. Ephesians 1:13-14 says very much the same thing and Ephesians 4:30 speaks again of the Christian having been sealed with the Spirit and, in this verse, it gives the period of that sealing - it is, *"...until the day of redemption."* The Christian can be forever secure in their salvation upon the basis of this sealing of the Christian by the Spirit.

12. The Christian's position in Christ

The Christian is united with Christ, by the Spirit, to the extent that they are said to be *"...in Christ."* This close identification with Christ means the Christian is forever accepted by God - who sees the Christian as *"...clothed...with Christ"* (Gal 3:27). The Christian's position *"...in Christ..."* is a work of God for humanity. In 1 Corinthians 1:30, it says, *"It is because of Him* (God) *that you are in Christ Jesus..."* Having placed the Christian *"...in Christ"* 2 Corinthians 1:21, *"Now it is God who makes both us and you stand firm in Christ."* It is God who places the Christian in Christ, it is God who causes the Christian to remain (stand firm) in Christ and it is God who accepts the Christian because of their position *"...in Christ."* Saved by grace, kept by grace.

Conclusion

The truth of safe-keeping through grace is revealed through:

> 1. The purposes of God in grace, are not fulfilled at initial salvation, making it necessary for God to keep the saved Christian by ongoing grace for His purposes to be fulfilled.

> 2. The many provisions and safeguards which God has made, including Himself, His Son and the Holy Spirit, for the purpose of keeping safe the Christian.

Salvation by grace is the purpose of God's redemption through Christ. Failure to trust in Christ alone is seen when salvation is supposed to depend on anything other than believing in Christ, or when a Christian's security in salvation is made to depend at any point on their own effort or contribution.

The Christian contributes nothing to being saved and nothing to being kept saved.

It is all a work of God for humanity - and that's Good News!

Chapter 3

The doctrine of repentance

Modern teaching

For many Christians today repentance generally includes some or all of these elements: it is initiated by a person, it is done to draw a response from God, it is repeatedly carried out, it is being and/or saying sorry, it is making a commitment to strive never to commit a particular sin again and may often include paying back or making up for the wrong done. Modern teaching often includes that the failure to repent may be responsible for some problems or hard times encountered by a Christian.

All these teachings have, indisputably, been lifted straight out of the Old Covenant and applied to the Christian. This new understanding of repentance differs significantly from the definition and practice established in the Old Covenant. The Bible's teachings on New Covenant repentance offer a clear understanding that alleviates any burdens caused by misunderstandings. When properly understood, these teachings restore joy and security to the Christian's salvation and deepen their love for God through Jesus.

New Testament repentance

Acts 5:31 says, *"God exalted Him* (Jesus) *to His own right hand as Prince and Saviour that He might* **give repentance** *and forgiveness of sins to Israel."* The first reference to repentance outside the Gospels speaks of repentance being a gift from God to humanity. This Scripture shows that God is the initiator of New

Testament repentance, contrasting sharply with the Old Testament's approach to repentance.

Acts 11:18 also makes the point that New Testament repentance is initiated by God. It says, *"When they heard this* (that the Holy Spirit had been given to the Gentiles), *they had no further objections and praised God saying, '**God has granted** even the Gentiles **repentance** unto life.'"* New Testament repentance is something granted by God. In the whole of the Gospel of Jesus Christ, the emphasis is upon what God has done for humanity. This Scripture shows that this is true in this fundamental matter of repentance.

In the Old Testament, repentance was something done by a person to draw a response from God. In the New Testament, the order is reversed. Romans 2:4 says, *"Or do you show contempt for the riches of His* (God's) *kindness, forbearance and patience, not realising that **God's kindness is intended to lead you to repentance**."* Now the order is that God does something and the person responds. It is God's kindness that leads a person to respond to God, and that response is called repentance. The Apostle Paul writes, in 2 Timothy 2:25, of how repentance is something granted by God: *"Instead, he must gently instruct his opponents, in the hope that **God will grant** them repentance leading to a knowledge of the truth."*

The writer of the letter to the Hebrews says in Hebrews 6:1, *"...repentance from acts that lead to death..."* is a foundation of the Christian Gospel. So, what is it that, in the Gospel of God's grace, will lead to death? It is legalism – which centres around self-effort - which, in a Covenant of Grace, leads to death. Hebrews 10:26-29, *"How much more severely do you think a man deserves to be punished who has trampled the Son of God under foot, who has treated as an unholy thing the blood of the covenant which sanctified him, and who has insulted the Spirit of Grace."* That insult to the Spirit of Grace occurs when a person believes their own effort can make them, or help make/keep them, right with God. It is that, self-effort, from which a person must repent because such an attitude leads to death – to eternal separation from God.

Hebrews 6:4,6 says, *"It is impossible for those who have once been enlightened...if they fall away, to be brought back to repentance."* So, contrary to the Old Testament concept of repeated acts of repentance, the Bible says that in the New Testament; it is impossible to repent a second time having once repented and then fallen away. This *"falling away"* refers to a falling away from faith in Christ, not a falling away in terms of a sinful lifestyle.

So, to summarise the major teachings on repentance in the New Testament: it is a gift from Jesus, it is granted by God, it is a person's response to God's kindness, it is a foundation of the Christian faith, and it is a one-off event. That totally separates New Testament repentance from Old Testament repentance.

Jesus' teachings on repentance

When Jesus came, He called upon people to repent and He taught about repentance. When Jesus sent out His disciples, He told them to go and preach that people should repent. Repentance is a major theme of the Gospel and as the writer of the Hebrews says, it is a foundation of the Christian faith. In His teachings, Jesus gives His definition of repentance.

The Lost Sheep

In Luke 15 three parables revolve around the issue of repentance. In the first parable, Jesus tells of a shepherd with 100 sheep, one of which is lost and ninety-nine of which are not lost. The shepherd searches for, and finds the lost sheep. The shepherd then carries the lost sheep back home and, finally, invites his neighbours together to share his joy over the sheep being found. Jesus then says, in Luke 15:7, *"I tell you that in the same way there will be more rejoicing in heaven over one sinner who repents than over ninety-nine righteous persons who do not need to repent."* Jesus draws a clear comparison between the one lost sheep and the one repentant sinner and between the ninety-nine sheep which are not lost and the ninety-nine persons who did not need to repent.

Jesus says that the sequence of events which the lost sheep went through is *"…in the same way…"* the path for a repentant sinner. In order then to understand Jesus' definition of repentance, an answer is required to the question, "What did the lost sheep do that allows Jesus to liken it to a repentant sinner?" In the sequence of events in the parable, the first active part played by the sheep was that it got lost. All the other events affecting the sheep were initiated and carried through by the shepherd. The shepherd did the searching, the shepherd did the finding, the shepherd did the lifting and the carrying and, finally, the shepherd gathered his neighbours to share his joy. Throughout that sequence of events, at the end of the story, Jesus says that the lost sheep is like a repentant sinner.

The sheep does make a second contribution to the sequence of events which leads to it being restored to its home. Initially, *the sheep gets lost*; subsequently, *the sheep accepts being found*. It allows the shepherd to carry it home on his shoulders. Without the sheep's consent, the shepherd would not have been able to lift and carry a full-grown sheep. So, the sheep got lost and then accepted being found. That, Jesus says, is repentance in the New Testament. The Christian accepts that they are lost - that is why the Christian first turns to Jesus and accepts Him as Lord and Saviour. New Testament repentance requires one other thing - that the lost one should accept that they have been found and that it is the responsibility, and joy, of the Shepherd to carry the Christian safe home, all the way to Glory.

There is no room in Jesus' story and definition for any concept of the repentant sinner contributing anything towards their salvation or their restoration. There is no requirement for striving not to get lost again, no requirement for contrition or sorrow, no suggestion of any burden or responsibility being placed upon, or accepted by, the repentant one at any point. How different from the Old Testament where the burden was squarely upon the sinner to get right with God. Now it is God who makes a person right with Himself. It should be noted that it is the shepherd's joy to carry the burden of the lost sheep until it is safe back home: *"...he joyfully puts it on his shoulders and goes home."* It is Jesus' joy to carry the responsibility for (1) the salvation of the lost sinner, (2) the safe-keeping of that now-saved Christian within the family of God and, eventually, (3) their welcome into Glory.

The Lost Coin

The second parable, the parable of the lost coin, illustrates the same points. It is the coin which is lost. The woman does the cleaning and the searching until the coin is found and restored. Again, Jesus likens that lost coin to a repentant sinner. So, again, the question must be asked, "What does the coin do that allows Jesus to liken it to a repentant sinner?" As with the lost sheep, the answer to that question is that the coin became lost and then was found. The coin contributed nothing to the sequence of events. The initiative and responsibility for locating and restoring the coin lay entirely with the woman. Just as with Christians, the initiative and responsibility for their salvation and restoration lies entirely with God - accepting that truth is, according to the teachings of Christ, New Testament repentance.

The challenging aspect for Christians is not acknowledging their lostness. Every Christian has gone through this realization before accepting Jesus as their Savior. In fact, it is recognizing their need for a Savior that ultimately leads them to accept Him. The challenging aspect for Christians is accepting their found status and recognizing that it is God's responsibility to restore them, both to the family of God and eventually to Glory.Christians are tempted to believe (and is often taught) that they must make some contribution to the process, once they are found. In the face of such temptation Christians should remember the lost sheep and the lost coin. A Christian can feel that their lifestyle is such that after being saved, they are still a burden to Jesus. The Christian should remember, at such times, how Jesus taught of the joy with which the shepherd placed the sheep on his shoulders and carried it all the way home and then, still rejoicing, called together his neighbours to celebrate.

The Christian should allow Jesus to be the burden-bearer – that is Christ's joy, to safeguard His flock right into Glory.

Repentance as taught to the Jews required them to contribute to the process of their salvation; repentance as taught by Jesus makes no such demand of the Christian.

The Lost Son

The third parable in Luke 15 is the parable of the lost son - often referred to as the parable of the prodigal son. The son leaves home, squanders his inheritance, comes upon hard times, thinks of a way of saving himself and sets off back to his father's house. In Luke 15:18-19 the son is turning homeward, *"I will set out and go back to my father and say to him: Father, I have sinned against heaven and against you. I am no longer worthy to be called your son; make me like one of your hired servants."* Sadly, many Christians understand, and may even have been taught, this "turning back to the father" – including turning away from his sinful life - is the son repenting.

In fact, the young man is far from repentance at this point. He is going home with a plan which will allow him to be the author of his own salvation. He is to become like a hired man. In other words, he will work for his father and, that way, he will be able to pay his father back the money he has had and squandered. There is, at this point, no recognition by the son of his need for grace. There is, at this point, no understanding by the son that the father is bothered not by the squandering of money but by the broken relationship between himself and his son.

So, the son sets off home.

The next sequence of events is initiated by the father. The son contributes nothing. The father sees the son coming, rushes out to meet him, throws his arms around the son and kisses him. This is not the welcome the son was expecting. The father asks no questions about the inheritance. He makes no demands for repayment. He awaits no expression of sorrow from the son. The father simply extends, unconditionally and very publicly, a father's love for his son.

In verse 21, the son speaks to the father, and there is a marked difference between what he planned to say (in verse 19) and what he actually says. The son says, "*Father I have sinned against heaven and against you. I am no longer worthy to be called your son.*" The son, in the face of overwhelming love, drops any idea of working for his father. He now understands that it is the broken relationship which is the issue between him and his father - it is not the squandered inheritance. He acknowledges, rightly so, his unworthiness to be called a son. However, he then experiences true repentance—this means he recognizes that he was lost but has now been found. He accepts the freely offered gift of unconditional restoration to sonship. That acceptance is demonstrated in the subsequent verses in the passage.

The Greek word used for repentance in the New Testament is metanoia, which means "to change course after further insight." The son in this story perfectly illustrates this. He came home with one course of action planned. He received further insight into the real issue through his father's demonstration of love. He then changed course, away from self-effort and towards total dependence upon an undeserved, and unconditional, free offer of salvation and restoration to sonship.

That is the same undeserved and unconditional offer that God extends to every human being: restoration through Jesus, allowing for full sonship. Many Christians are still rooted in verse 19, acknowledging their lostness but still depending on their own efforts. As a result, they are essentially functioning as servants rather than embracing their identity as sons. The glory of understanding God's grace, and understanding repentance, is that it moves the Christians from verse 19 to verse 21 - from servanthood to sonship. The Christian, to ascertain their understanding of repentance, should ask themselves the question, "Am I in some way working for God (verse 19) as though I can pay Him back for the wrong I have done, or working to prove my gratitude for salvation or am I simply receiving from God (verse 21) what He is freely offering - even though I recognise I do not deserve such a gift?"

The sheep, the coin, the son - none of them did any of the things required under Old Testament repentance. Jesus teaches a new understanding of repentance. The Christian must make certain that they are living under New Testament repentance. The repentance Jesus teaches cannot happen without faith in Christ and, equally, faith in Christ, as God's provision for the lost, is New Testament repentance. So, in the New Testament, faith and repentance became a single issue.

Jesus' teachings demonstrated

When considering the following illustrations of Jesus' teachings on repentance, it is important to remember that forgiveness of sins, justification or whatever other words are used to show a right relationship with God cannot come without repentance. So, if the New Testament Scriptures talk of sins being forgiven, or justification taking place, then repentance must also have taken place.

Matthew 21:28-32: The two sons

A man has two sons. He asks one to go and work in the vineyard and the son replies that he will not. Later he changes his mind and goes. The father asks the second son to work in the vineyard. The second son says he will go, but then he fails to do so. Which son, Jesus asked His listeners, did what the father wanted. The chief priests and the elders answered that the first son did the father's will.

If their answer is correct, then, Jesus is teaching salvation by works and that it is only by doing what God asks that Christians carry out the Father's will. Old Testament repentance was turning away from sin (in this case the defying of the father) and turning to the things of God (in this case, obedience to the father). That is what is illustrated by the first son. There is no grace in the relationship between the son and his father, the relationship is based upon works.

With the second son, one can truly see the Christian. Here is a young man whose immediate response is to say "Yes" to his father; but who subsequently fails to live out his initial intent. Is not that the position of every Christian? Does not the Christian's heart cry "Yes" when they hear the Father's voice - and does not that Christian's sinful flesh often act as a barrier and so stop them from fulfilling their heart's desire to serve God?

The relationship between the second son and his father must depend upon grace; the relationship between the Christian and God must equally depend upon grace. Contrary to much modern teaching, it is the second son who does the father's will - albeit only in his initial heart response. The battle between the flesh and the spirit goes on; but the immediate response of the Christian to their Father's voice should never be, as it was with the first son, "No, I will not do what you ask." The Christian says "Yes" and then fails. This story shows that New Testament repentance is about the heart's intent towards obedience not, as with Old Testament repentance, a series of works and outward acts. Heart intent is sufficient in the New Covenant because God's grace covers all the times the Christian's heart says, "Yes," but their old, sinful nature presents them following through.

Mark 2:1-12: The paralytic

A paralytic is brought to Jesus. The friends of the paralytic are so determined to get their friend to Jesus that they lower him through the roof. The passage says, *"When Jesus saw their faith, He said to the paralytic, 'Son, your sins are forgiven.'"* Something which has already occurred in the passage constitutes repentance because, without repentance there can be no forgiveness of sins. What did the paralytic do that Jesus accepted as repentance? The passage provides the answer in that it says Jesus responded to their faith. The paralytic, and his friends, saw the hopelessness of his situation, accepted his lostness, and came to the only one who could do anything to change the situation. Faith in Jesus, that He can do for the Christian what the Christian cannot do for themself is, under the New Testament as clearly illustrated in this story: repentance. There are no promises from the paralytic, and there are no questions or conditions from Jesus; He simply saw the paralytic's faith, which demonstrated his repentance, and forgave him.

Luke 13:1-3: The murdered worshippers

In this short passage, a group of Galileans are murdered by Roman soldiers whilst they are in the Temple offering sacrifices to God. Does not what Christians _do_ for God demonstrate repentance? Apparently not, for Jesus warns the people to whom He is talking, *"Unless you repent you too will all perish."* Those who believe that a good life, with modern day "sacrifices," represents repentance are mistaken. Repentance is faith in God and His provision for us in Jesus. It is faith, not lifestyle, that counts in the New Testament.

Luke 17: 3-4: Self-effort of heart intent?

Jesus, here, instructs His followers that if anyone sins against them, even seven times a day (a term meaning "many times," not literally limited to seven) and on each occasion says, "I repent," then the sinner is to be forgiven. Such a teaching suggests that repentance cannot involve any kind of effort on the part of the person. Jesus teaches that if a person repeatedly sins each day, it does not affect their entitlement to forgiveness if they say, "I repent."

How many people would accept that another has repented when the sinning continues unabated? Much modern teaching states that repentance involves turning away from sin, but where is that in this teaching from Christ? Much modern teaching has Christians believing that repentance involves striving never to repeat a sin, but where is that in this teaching? Both ideas are absent from the teachings of Christ because they represent Old Testament repentance. However, with the understanding that New Testament repentance means accepting one's lostness and accepting being found - that is, the receiving of the undeserved gift of forgiveness and reconciliation, then this teaching of Christ makes sense.

It should be noted that this teaching relates to repentance and forgiveness that can happen multiple times between two people and should not be confused with the repentance and forgiveness which occurs as a once-off event between an individual and God.

Luke 18:9-14: The Pharisee and the tax collector

In this parable, told by Jesus, the Pharisee is very sure of his righteousness. It is based on all that he has done or not done. He is not a robber, an evildoer, or an adulterer. He fasts and tithes. He gives thanks to God that he is such a man. The tax collector, though, will not even look up to pray. He simply confesses the hopelessness of his sinful self. Jesus teaches that it is the tax collector who goes home justified. As there can be no justification without repentance, what the tax collector did and/or said must constitute New Testament repentance. What the tax collector did is entirely in keeping with the rest of Christ's teaching on repentance. The tax collector accepted his lostness and accepted that God was the only one who could change that situation.

New Testament repentance involves acknowledging one's lostness and accepting mercy from the only One who can change the situation through that mercy.

Luke 18:18-29: The rich ruler

Here is a man who has made great efforts to keep right with God. He has kept the Commandments since he was a boy, yet still has no assurance of his salvation. Far from encouraging him, Jesus puts to the rich young ruler a demand that cultural expectations make it impossible to meet. The ruler goes away unhappy. He is still not right with God, and God has set him a standard that he simply cannot meet.

A rich man will give to the poor, build synagogues, tithe his possessions and meet many requirements of the Law. The poor people hearing this, and realising the rich man was not right with God, will have thought (vs 26), "If the rich, with all their opportunities to please God, cannot get into heaven, then who can be saved?" Jesus is pointing out to the people the utter hopelessness of their situation. He is pointing them to total dependence on a Saviour. He is pointing them away from their lifestyle and works and towards a God of grace. He is calling them to repent.

Luke 23:42-43: The dying thief

The thief, dying on the cross alongside Jesus, offers Christ nothing but his faith. Jesus assures the thief that, on that very day, he will enter Paradise with Christ. If repentance is not an integral, and inseparable, part of faith then upon what basis did Jesus give His assurance to the thief; for without repentance, there can be no forgiveness of sin? In these closing scenes of Jesus' crucifixion, He demonstrates the principle of New Testament repentance which He had repeatedly taught. That is, in the New Testament, the repentant sinner is one who comes empty-handed to God, recognising their lostness, recognising they can never change that lostness, and ready to accept God's freely offered, unconditional salvation and restoration - to accept being found.

Conclusion

Repentance as something which a person does as a contribution, in addition to faith, towards the gaining or keeping of their salvation has no Scriptural basis under the New Testament.

Repentance, viewed as an act a person undertakes to reconcile with God, is an Old Testament concept that has no relevance in the life of a Christian. This perspective can make repentance feel like a burden, particularly for those who are struggling in their faith, and it ultimately does not bring glory to Jesus. Therefore, such a teaching should be strongly resisted. Jesus teaches, and demonstrates, that faith and repentance are integral and inseparable parts of the same act. A person cannot repent without first having faith in Jesus as their Saviour and, conversely, a person cannot have faith without repenting. The two go hand in hand. They are not separate issues.

Jesus teaches and demonstrates that New Testament repentance is the acceptance of being lost and, equally, the acceptance of being found: in other words, the acceptance of God's freely offered grace. Repentance, in the New Testament, has become a total dependence on God and what He has done for humanity.

Chapter 4

The doctrine of forgiveness

Modern teaching

Under the Old Covenant, every time a person needed to be forgiven, they would bring the necessary sacrifice to the priest who would offer the sacrifice and make atonement: once that was done, God forgave.

So, Old Covenant forgiveness was an often-repeated event, initiated by the sinner, carried through by the priest and then responded to by God.

Modern teaching on forgiveness can often carry the same kind of Old Covenant message in that, it is a process the sinner initiates, is an often-repeated process and one to which God then responds.

Modern teaching on forgiveness requires modern "sacrifices" to replace the Old Covenant sacrifices of an animal or bird. Today's sacrifices that must be brought to God to ensure His forgiveness of the Christian's sins, as many are incorrectly taught include that a Christian must:

Confess their sin(s). This may be based on 1 John 1:9, *"If we confess our sins, He (God) is faithful and just and will forgive us our sins..."*

First forgive others. This may be based on Matt 6:15, *"But if you do not forgive others their sins, your Father will not forgive your sins."*

Receive forgiveness on a moment-by-moment basis. This may be based on Luke 17:4, *"If someone sins against you seven times in a day, and seven times comes back to you and says, 'I repent' forgive them."*

Ask for forgiveness and is dependent upon the Christian having first forgiven others. This may be based upon Matt 6:12, *"Forgive us our sins as we have forgiven those who sin against us."*

Be baptised in order to be forgiven. This may be based upon Acts 2:38 in which Peter tells the crowd, *"Repent and be baptised every one of you in the name of Jesus Christ for the forgiveness of your sins."*

Receive forgiveness as an act of God's grace. There is no Scriptural basis for this belief. It is rooted in a misunderstanding of God's dealings with humanity and the general sense of unworthiness which so often burdens Christians.

Not one of these modern teachings applies to the Christian.

Christians are correctly taught that their sins were forgiven through Christ's sacrificial death by crucifixion. By believing in this truth, a person is saved and becomes a Christian.However, Christians are often also taught that there is a process of ongoing forgiveness which requires them, as they become aware of sin in their life, to request forgiveness for that latest sin.

Failing to seek forgiveness for known sins may lead to God, as most Christians are incorrectly taught, being displeased with that individual. Not to the extent that their salvation is necessarily at risk, but that their day-to-day relationship with God is negatively impacted. He will be less pleased with them because of the sin *and* the lack of a request for forgiveness for that sin and, therefore, He will be less willing to use them for Kingdom/Gospel purposes or to bless the Christian. This is all completely unbiblical teaching and thinking.

This leads to the Christians believing that their relationship with the Lord is not a stable one, except in the issue of ultimate salvation. Teaching the incorrect doctrine of ongoing forgiveness renders a Christian far less effective for the Gospel than they could be. It causes a sense of unworthiness, even failure, in Christians as they are taught that God may be displeased with them. For the Christian who takes this incorrect teaching too much to heart, there is a risk that they will begin to feel that, perhaps, even their salvation is at stake.

This incorrect teaching can cripple Christians spiritually and practically in their ability to live out the Gospel.

It's not hard to see that this incorrect teaching has its roots in the Old Covenant and, consequently, has no place in the lives of those living under the New Covenant, that is, Christians.

What is forgiveness?

One of the problems with a Christian's understanding of forgiveness is that there is a tendency to misuse the word in everyday conversation.

When a person asks someone else to forgive them, the word is generally being used in the context of, "I am apologising for what I have just done/said." It can also be used to mean, "Please don't be angry at me." Another common use of the word is to convey the message, "Please overlook the offence."

These modern misunderstandings of the meaning of forgiveness can be carried over into a Christian's understanding of how God deals with sin and how God deals with Christians. Christians can often, in effect, be saying to God, "I am apologising for what I have done; please don't be angry with me. Please overlook the offence." All of which are incorrect understandings of forgiveness.

Two essential elements. There are two common elements which must be involved in the appropriate use of the word "forgiveness." The two essential elements are: (1) the taking up of a burden created by someone else and (2) the giving up of any resentment towards the one who created the burden. So, when God says to humanity that He forgives their sins He is, in effect, saying, "I will bear the consequences of what you have done and I will not hold it against you." Such a statement, and understanding, contains the two elements of true forgiveness. Jesus takes up the burden created by people's sins - the burden of the death penalty and He does not hold that against those people. He still extends His love and blessings towards everyone.

So, when a person asks God for forgiveness, that person is saying to God, "Please accept the burden created by my sin and do not hold it against me." This, God did, in Jesus, in a one-off acceptance of the burden of sin for all humanity. The Old Covenant process of repeatedly asking for forgiveness has, incorrectly, become part of New Covenant teaching.

With the understanding of forgiveness laid out above, the foolishness, and inappropriateness, of repeatedly asking God to bear the consequences of our sins and not hold that against us can clearly be seen. There is only one possible answer God can give to such a request, "I already have borne the consequences of your sin – all of your sin – on the cross at Calvary. And I have never allowed that sacrifice I made to negatively impact upon My relationship with you." Every time a Christian asks for forgiveness, that is the only response God can give. Forgiveness is a "done deal." Hebrews 10:10, *"...we have been made holy through the sacrifice of the body of Jesus Christ once for all."*

The most profound demonstration of forgiveness is the cross of Calvary. On that cross, Jesus Christ accepted into Himself the penalty, the consequences, the burden, for the sins every person has ever committed, or will ever commit, and He did not, and does not, hold that against the sinner.

New Covenant forgiveness, correctly understood in this way, stands in sharp contrast to Old Covenant forgiveness. No longer person-initiated, no longer person-centred, and no longer often repeated. At Calvary, it was God who initiated forgiveness by providing the sacrifice. It was God who was, and is, continually at the centre of the act of forgiveness as, in Jesus, He Himself became the means of atonement, and it is a "once for all" act which was concluded around 2,000 years ago.

Any teaching, therefore, that the Christian still needs to bring sacrifices - which today would be the asking for forgiveness, the forgiving of others, the confession of sin etc. - to receive forgiveness, is completely wrong, has no Scriptural basis and such a teaching is to imply that faith in the sacrifice of Christ is insufficient to make the Christian eternally right with God.

The Christian's relationship with God

A Christian has, through Christ, been reconciled to God: 2 Cor 5:18 says, *"God was reconciling the world to Himself in Christ, not counting men's sins against them."* The barrier of sin which once stood between God and humanity was dealt with by Jesus at the cross of Calvary. Now, through faith and by God's grace, Christians are brought into a familial relationship with God, receiving the position and rights of His children. That relationship starts at the moment of conversion and continues uninterrupted for eternity.

The relationship with God is one which He offers to every Christian as an outworking of His grace towards those who believe the Gospel message. This means that the relationship offered must be based on a fundamental truth of grace - which is that it is freely and undeservedly given. This means *the relationship exists <u>and continues</u> without regard to sin* – because sin has been dealt with, once and for all, on Calvary's cross.

A relationship with God can only commence once every question of sin has been dealt with. God will never compromise His holiness. God cannot be in relationship with someone who is still guilty of offences against Him. God accomplished this for humanity at the cross of Christ. The reason a Christian can have a relationship with God is because Jesus, on the cross, took into Himself, all the sins of all humanity forever. John the Baptist testified, *"Look, the Lamb of God who takes away the sin of the world"* (John 1:29). The Christian's sins have been taken away from them.

In 1 John 2:2, it states that it is not only the sins of the Christian that were taken away but, *"...the sins of the whole world."* Faith in the blood of Christ reconciles the Christian to God. Nothing can ever break that relationship. It is guaranteed by the Holy Spirit. Ephesians 1:13-14 says, *"...having believed, you were marked in Him with a seal, the promised Holy Spirit, who is a deposit guaranteeing our inheritance..."*

Therefore, with every question of sin dealt with by Jesus' sacrifice, *"...once for all,"* forgiveness cannot be given on a moment-by-moment basis – otherwise, the Christian's relationship with God would be equally "on and off." Sadly, that is exactly the kind of relationship which many Christians do have with God. Forgiveness was achieved for the Christian by Jesus. He bore the guilt for the Christians and took away all their sins and does not hold the Christian's sins against them.

The Christian's relationship with God, being based upon a fundamental truth of grace - that it is freely and undeservedly given - means; in keeping with the true nature of God's grace, *the relationship exists <u>and continues</u> without regard to the response*.

The Christian's relationship with God cannot depend, in any way at all, on anything that the Christian does for God. If it does, then, it would mean that a Christian's relationship with God is not based upon His grace, but on a mixture of His grace and the Christian's works. Grace must be totally free of obligation to remain grace. Therefore forgiveness, without which the Christian cannot be in relationship with God, cannot depend on anything the Christian does. The incorrect teachings about the need to confess sin, forgive others, ask for forgiveness and so on, as something a person needs to do to be forgiven, place that person in a works-oriented relationship with God. Such an understanding stands opposed to Scripture which states, *"For it is by grace you have been saved, through faith - and this not from yourselves, it is the gift of God - not by works, so that no one can boast"* (Ephesians 2:8-9).

The Christian's relationship with God is based solely on what Christ has achieved for humanity. In Him, the Christian is made right with God. It is Christ's achievement, freely given to the Christian, that makes the Christian acceptable to God. Nothing the Christian does or does not do, can affect their standing before God. Therefore forgiveness, which is necessary for the relationship with God to start, must be dependent only on faith in Christ and His achievement on behalf of the Christian. This reinforces the point that the Christian is forgiven once and for all time. The Christian is forgiven of all sins at the moment of coming to faith in Christ.

New Testament teaching on forgiveness

The following Scriptures show that under the New Covenant, forgiveness is now a Christ-initiated, and Christ-oriented aspect of the Christian's relationship with God.

Forgiveness is a debt cancelled. Matthew 18:23-27. The King in this story is owed a large amount of money. The debtor is unable to pay the debt. The man who owes the money seeks to be the author of his own salvation in that he offers in verse 26 to pay back the king the debt that is owed. However, in verse 27, the king illustrates the message of the Gospel by recognizing that the man cannot repay his debt. Instead of accepting the man's offer, the king cancels the debt altogether. The King accepted the burden created by the debtor and took the loss of the money, and we know the king did not hold it against the man because, after cancelling the debt, the king let the man go.

Forgiveness depends upon what Jesus has done for humanity. Matthew 26:28. Jesus, when instructing His followers at the last supper, said to them, *"This is My blood of the Covenant which is poured out for many for the* *forgiveness of sins.*" Forgiveness, in the New Covenant, comes through the blood of Christ. A person contributes nothing towards it. It is impossible to add to, or take away from, the achievement of the blood of the Lamb. Understanding this truth should bring a Christian into a more stable, constant relationship with God. When a Christian realizes they are completely forgiven, and that through the blood of Jesus, they can better experience the joy of their salvation. (See also: Ephesians 1:7)

Forgiveness is given as the result of faith - not a separate issue. Mark 2:1-12. The paralytic in this story was carried to Jesus by his friends and lowered through the roof. The passage says that *"When Jesus saw their faith He said to the paralytic, 'Son, your sins are forgiven.'"* At this point, the paralytic and his friends have demonstrated only faith. The Scripture confirms that: *"When Jesus saw their faith...."* If forgiveness of sins depends upon anything other than faith then Jesus had no right to respond to their faith by pronouncing the man's sins forgiven. Jesus responded to their faith, and He responded to the Christian's faith - not their deeds or contributions. Forgiveness does not depend on the Christian doing something, but on the Christian believing something.

Forgiveness is given through faith. Luke 7:36-50: This is the story of the woman at the house of Simon the Pharisee. The woman, in serving Jesus, makes up for the shortcomings and deliberate rudeness of Simon towards Jesus. She demonstrates a great love for Jesus and carries out acts of service which involve her own humiliation before those present. In verse 48, Jesus tells the woman, *"Your sins are forgiven."* It is not the acts of service, though, which have brought that forgiveness, for in verse 50, Jesus says to the woman, *"Your faith has saved you."* Christians must proclaim the truth that forgiveness comes through faith in Jesus - not through even costly acts of humiliating service, as carried out by this woman. It is through faith, and faith alone, that a person is made right with God.

Forgiveness empowers service. Luke 7:41-43, 47-48: Jesus, in the same incident at Simon's house, tells Simon a parable about two debtors. One owes a large amount, and the other owes a smaller amount. The one who is owed the money cancels the debt of both men because neither can pay back their debt. Jesus asks, "Who will love the forgiving creditor more?" Simon answers correctly that the one who had the bigger debt cancelled will love the more. When a Christian realises that ALL their sins are forgiven, that the Christian has a "clean sheet" with God from the first moment of salvation, then that Christian will love God more. That is the teaching of Scripture. The greater the awareness of forgiveness, the greater the love for the one forgiving.

Jesus then tells Simon that He knows the woman's sins are forgiven because she has shown much, and costly, love. In verse 48, Jesus says to the woman, *"Your sins are forgiven."* In Greek, that sentence is written in the perfect passive sense. What that means is that Jesus is recognising in the woman a present condition resulting from a past action. In other words, Jesus is saying, "I know you have received forgiveness for your sins because I can see the great love you have shown Me." <u>A present condition resulting from something that has already occurred</u>. Both the parable of the two debtors and Jesus' conversation with the woman highlight a crucial point: receiving forgiveness empowers Christians to perform acts of service—sometimes even at a personal cost—because of the love they have for the One who forgives. Jesus said, *"He who has been forgiven little loves little."* Little love brings little service. Let all Christians receive the freely offered forgiveness of God and, through the power of their greater love for the One who forgives, go on and serve the One who died to be able to give that forgiveness.

Forgiveness is a gift. Luke 15:11-24: In this story of the prodigal son, the father demonstrates New Covenant forgiveness. On seeing the son returning, the father humiliates himself by running through the village to meet the son. In the Middle East, no man would consider running in public as it is considered undignified. This father, though, is thinking only of his son. The father asks no questions of the son, makes no demands of the son, puts no conditions upon the son, and gives no rebuke to the son. The father overwhelms the son with love and a free offer of restoration to sonship. The son had come back with the attitude of a servant - he was going to work for his father to pay back the debt he owed his father. Receiving freely offered forgiveness changed the young man from a servant to a son. It does the same for the Christian. The father bore the burden created by his son and did not hold that against the son. That is New Covenant forgiveness.

Forgiveness is a work of God for humanity, not of humanity for God. Luke 18:9-14: The Pharisee more than kept The Law. He was a man more than dedicated to doing what God required. The Law required that the Pharisee fast once a week - this Pharisee fasted twice a week. The Law required a tenth of agricultural produce - this Pharisee gave a tenth of everything he had. The tax collector offered no such strivings or good works to God. He simply asked God to have mercy on him — the phrase used in the Scriptures literally means, "Lord, make atonement for me." The tax collector went home justified, as Jesus said. His sins were forgiven not because of anything the tax collector contributed, but through the atoning sacrifice of Christ. The only thing that mattered was the faith he had in God to do for him what he could not do for himself.

Forgiveness does not depend upon what a person does. Luke 23:24. As Jesus was being nailed to the cross, He prayed, *"Father, forgive them, for they do not know what they are doing."* To understand forgiveness correctly, the question must be asked, "By what right did Jesus ask the Father to forgive His murderers?" It was a murder because the High Priest, the Pharisees and the Romans all knew that Jesus had, in the words of Pontius Pilate, committed no crime that warranted the death penalty. If much of modern teaching on forgiveness is correct then Jesus had no right to ask the Father to forgive His murderers. They had not confessed to their act as a sin, they had not asked for forgiveness nor had they expressed any sorrow for their actions. None of the things which many Christians are told are necessary before God will grant forgiveness.

The reason Jesus did have a right to make that request of His Father was because He was about to accept into Himself the consequences of His murderers' actions and He was not holding that against them - and those are the two elements of true forgiveness. Forgiveness is never deserved - as this Scripture clearly shows. Forgiveness is a work of God for humanity, not the other way around. Forgiveness is freely offered and faith opens the Christian up to receive what is offered. Nailed to the cross by a jeering, Christ-rejecting crowd, He prays for His murderers, *"Father, forgive them."* That is true New Covenant forgiveness. It is Christ bearing the burden of humanity's sins and not holding it against them. By the grace of God, that same freely offered, undeserved forgiveness is still available to all today who will believe.

Forgiveness is given through faith in Jesus and that alone. Luke 23:42-43: Surely one of the clearest examples of forgiveness through faith, and faith alone, must be the thief dying on the cross alongside Jesus. The thief did absolutely nothing except to place his hope and faith in Jesus Christ. That was sufficient for Jesus to reassure him of his salvation - which entails and includes his forgiveness. If a declaration of faith was sufficient for the thief, it must be sufficient for all people.

Forgiveness is a gift from God. Acts 5:31. *"God exalted Him* (Jesus) *to His own right hand as Prince and Saviour that He might GIVE repentance and forgiveness of sins to Israel."* Forgiveness is a gift from Jesus. A gift is free. A gift is not contributed towards, not earned and not deserved; it is simply a gift. Jesus is the only One who can offer forgiveness of sins because it was He who bore the consequences of everyone's sins. Since Calvary, He has been saying to everyone, "I have borne the consequences of what you have done and I do not hold that against you." People are required only to believe the Good News.

Forgiveness depends only upon faith. Acts 10:43. This Scripture makes plain the simple truth that forgiveness comes through faith in Christ, and that alone. The need for ongoing forgiveness is not a burden to be carried by the Christian. An understanding of forgiveness makes it one of the sources of joy in a Christian's life and relationship with God. Another gift! This Scripture says, *"All the prophets testify about Him* (Jesus) *that everyone who believes in Him receives forgiveness of sins through His name."* Faith and forgiveness are not separate issues. If a Christian has faith in Jesus, that Christian is forgiven. This right understanding reinforces the central truth of Christian teaching which is that faith, and faith alone, is all that is required of anyone by God. (See also: Acts 13:38-39).

Forgiveness is not contributed to by a person in any way. Colossians 2:13. This Scripture says, *"When you were dead in your sins and in the uncircumcision of your sinful nature, God made you alive with Christ. He forgave us all our sins...."* This makes it clear that forgiveness is something God has done for everyone. It is important to stress this point because so much of what is taught as the Gospel reverses this emphasis and stresses what a person should be doing for God. Such teaching is neither the Gospel nor Good News and makes Christ's burden heavy, contrary to His own words, in Matt 11:30, *"...My burden is light."* Wrong teaching has caused their faith to be a heavy burden for many Christians. Forgiveness in the New Covenant is a source of great joy for the Believer.

Forgiveness is dependent upon the shedding of blood. Hebrews 9:22. *"In fact, The Law requires that nearly everything be cleansed with blood, and without the shedding of blood there is no forgiveness."* Those who teach that forgiveness is dependent upon a contribution from the sinner overlook this Scripture and have a cheap and easy forgiveness. God has always demanded a blood sacrifice for sins. Forgiveness of sins does not come on the basis of a prayer request, nor on the basis of a confession of sin, nor on the basis of expressing sorrow. Forgiveness does not come on the basis of making every effort not to sin again, nor on the basis of any other of these modern days sacrifices that Christians are often encouraged to bring to God. Forgiveness is granted on the basis of shed blood. For the Israelites that meant animal sacrifices, but for Christians it means the blood of Christ. It is that, and that alone, that allows God to forgive a person's sins. This Scripture shows that God made forgiveness available to all nearly 2,000 years ago when the blood was shed, and not daily as the sin occurs. Christ is not shedding His blood today. Forgiveness is no longer an issue between God and the Christian. As Christ proclaimed, *"It is finished."* In 1 John 2:12, the Apostle writes, *"I write to you, dear children, because your sins have been forgiven on account of His name."* John uses the past tense; it has already happened.

Not understanding forgiveness as a past event leads to ineffectiveness for the Gospel. 2 Peter 1:5-9. Peter has been writing about the different qualities a Christian should seek to build up in their life. Peter writes that possession of these qualities, which include faith, goodness, knowledge, self-control and others leading up to love, will prevent a Christian from *"...being ineffective and unproductive in* (their) *knowledge of our Lord Jesus Christ."* In verse 9 Peter writes, *"But if anyone does not have them, they are nearsighted and blind, and have forgotten that he has been cleansed from their past sins."* Forgetting that forgiveness is a closed issue, forgetting that all sins have been forgiven, will cause a Christian to be ineffective for the Gospel. This will happen because the Christians will assume that their daily life continually creates a barrier between them and God. Such a Christian will not expect much from God and, as with Jesus in Nazareth, God's ability to work through such a Christian will be limited because of their lack of faith - not in God's power, but faith in their standing before God.

Forgiveness is justice, not grace. 1 John 1:9. Through lack of understanding many Christians think that God's forgiveness is an act of grace from Him to the Christian. It is not. This Scripture states clearly that when *"...we confess* (that is, agree with God) *our sins then He is faithful and JUST and will forgive us our sins..."* God will always punish sin. His grace is that He sent His Son to be the punishment bearer. Having thus punished Jesus in our stead, God in not punishing the believing sinners for their sins is simply acting in a just way. There is no punishment due the believing sinners, which is why they are not punished. It is fair, it is just, but it is not grace. Jesus is God's grace to humanity. This is more than any apparent semantics or splitting of hairs. It has to do with the Christian's basic attitude to forgiveness and, thus, to God. Forgiveness, for the Christian is a right, not an act of Divine mercy. Christians should be confident in what Christ has achieved for them. (Hebrews 4:16).

Two questions

Hebrews 10:1, *"The Law is only a shadow of the good things that are coming - not the realities themselves. For this reason, it can never, by the same sacrifices repeated endlessly year after year, make perfect those who draw near to worship."* The sacrifices offered to obtain forgiveness had to be endlessly repeated. Each new sin demanded a new sacrifice in order to receive new forgiveness - that is the declared way of things under the old Covenant of Moses.

Under the New Covenant, though, the Bible declares, in Hebrews 10:12-14, *"But when this priest (Jesus) had offered for all time one sacrifice for sins, He sat down at the right hand of God. Since that time, He waits for His enemies to be made his footstool, because by one sacrifice He has made perfect forever those who are being made holy."* What a joyful contrast to the Old Covenant! In Christ, and by Christ, the Christian has been made perfect in the sight of God. The Christian may not feel or think they are perfect, but the Word of God stands far above human feelings and thoughts. Repeated sacrifices brought no perfection, but the one sacrifice of Christ brings perfection to all who believed. So:

The first question is: If Christ has made the Christian perfect in the eyes of God, as the Bible says, then, how can the Christian continually need to be forgiven?

Col 1:22 says, *"But now He (God) has reconciled you by Christ's physical body through death to present you holy in His sight, without blemish and free from accusation."*

<u>The second question is</u>: If the Christian is free, through Christ, even from accusation, then how can the Christian possibly need to be forgiven of anything?

Conclusion

The contrast between Old Covenant and New Covenant forgiveness is clear:

Old Covenant forgiveness	New Covenant forgiveness
Repeated sacrifices	One sacrifice
The sinner provided the sacrifice	Christ provided the sacrifice
Works	Faith
The priest made atonement	Christ made atonement
Brought no perfection	Brings perfection
God forgave	God forgave

All the Scriptures listed (as well as many others), the death and resurrection of Jesus Christ, the indwelling Holy Spirit and the Christian's new, and eternal, relationship with God, all testify to the following truths about forgiveness in the New Covenant:

Forgiveness: is something done by God for humanity,
comes through faith, and faith, alone,
is a gift from God,
is a "once for all" event,
is an act of justice, not grace.

Only with such an understanding of forgiveness can the Scripture be true which says, Romans 5:1: *"Therefore, since we have been justified through faith, we have peace with God through our Lord Jesus Christ."*

Chapter 5

The doctrine of righteousness

The need to understand Biblical righteousness

Knowing and understanding New Covenant teachings on righteousness removes any sense of burden from Christians by showing that their right standing before God is eternally achieved and assured by Jesus Christ.

The writer of Hebrews declares that it is possible to be in the faith for a long time and yet still be spiritually immature and unfruitful. Hebrews 5:12 says, *"In fact, though by this time you ought to be teachers, you need someone to teach you the elementary truths of God's Word all over again. You need milk, not solid food."* Hebrews 5:13 gives the reason for this spiritual immaturity and lack of fruit, *"Anyone who lives on milk, being still an infant, is not acquainted with the teaching about righteousness."*

The results of not understanding the Bible's teachings on righteousness are spiritual immaturity and, therefore, lack of fruit for the Kingdom.

A Christian who lacks understanding of the Scriptures teaching on righteousness will constantly seek to achieve and maintain their own sense of righteousness and will, therefore, always remain spiritually immature and unfruitful.

A lack of understanding of the Bible's teachings on righteousness embeds spiritual immaturity and lack of fruit. These results in turn, potentially, create for the Christian, a "see-saw" relationship with God and could burden the

Christian with a sense of failure, heaviness, depression, and condemnation that can eventually cause a Christian to fall away completely from any attempt to live out their faith.

Old Covenant teachings on righteousness

The God-given righteousness of the Old Testament is illustrated through Abraham. Genesis 15:6, *"Abram believed the Lord, and He credited it to him as righteousness."* Abram (Abraham) had a righteousness of character, given to him by God. This righteousness was not a result of the way Abraham lived, but because of his faith in God's word and it was sufficient unto salvation.

In the same way, the Scriptures explain how others living under the Old Covenant obtained a righteousness that led to salvation. Galatians 3:7-9, *"Understand, then, that those who have faith are children of Abraham. Scripture foresaw that God would justify the Gentiles by faith and announced the gospel in advance to Abraham: "All nations will be blessed through you." So those who rely on faith are blessed along with Abraham, the man of faith."*

People of the Old Covenant who were trusting in and relying on God for their salvation – whilst not understanding the fullness of what that meant because Jesus had not been revealed – were counted righteous along with Abraham because they had turned away from trusting in and relying on an earned self-righteousness.

In the Bible, within the Old Covenant era, the "greats" of our faith (for example, Noah, Isaac, Jacob, Moses, Elijah, Elisha, David), the many prophets and all those trusting in God for their salvation, and not an earned righteousness which came through obedience to the Law, are often referred to as "righteous." This is a reference to their righteousness of character, given in response to their faith and sufficient unto salvation - as faith unto salvation was also sufficient for Abraham.

Jesus, when challenging the Sadducees about their lack of faith in the resurrection, confirms the fact of Abraham's and others' salvation in Matthew 22:32 when He quotes God as saying, *"I am the God of Abraham, the God of Isaac and the God of Jacob."* And Jesus goes on to say, *"He is not the God of the dead, but of the living."*

However, also within the Old Covenant era, the Pharisees and teachers of the Law came to teach that obedience to the Law was sufficient unto salvation and, after time, this became the accepted vehicle of salvation. Thus, faith was wrongly replaced by works. This was the understanding of salvation, and the religious belief, that prevailed when Jesus entered the world.

The apparent righteousness of men and women as taught in the Old Testament came through the Covenant of Moses. It was an earned righteousness which was determined entirely by a person's lifestyle and could, therefore, vary from moment to moment requiring sacrifices to make atonement for a person's sins. This righteousness was not given by God, was earned through lifestyle and, although it could give a certain appearance of right-standing before God, it was insufficient for salvation - for that, there had to be faith in salvation through God. Amongst many such Scriptures, Romans 3:20 makes clear, *"Therefore no one will be declared righteous in His sight by observing The Law; rather, through The Law we become conscious of sin."*

Righteousness is one area where it is clear to see the blending of Old and New Covenants. Christians know they must be saved by faith in Christ but many accept teaching that says their lifestyle contributes to the retention of that right standing before God.

New Covenant teachings on righteousness

In the New Covenant of Christ, God freely gives righteousness to a person in response to that person's faith in Christ – such faith also being a gift from God. This means that under the New Covenant, for the Christian, faith in Christ and eternal righteousness before God are one simultaneous event. As long as the Christian retains faith in Jesus, they retain righteousness in the eyes of God and, therefore, retain their salvation.

The *"...gift of righteousness..."* (Romans 5:17) under the New Covenant brings with it the gift of the Holy Spirit. Acts 2:38-39 says, *"Peter replied, 'Repent and be baptised, every one of you, in the name of Jesus Christ for the forgiveness of your sins. And you will receive the gift of the Holy Spirit. The promise is for you and your children and for all who are far off - for all whom the Lord our God will call.'"*

In response to the Christian's God-given faith in Christ—a faith sufficient for salvation—it is the Holy Spirit who indwells the believer and works His righteousness from within, transforming the inner life into outwardly righteous living. Romans 8:11 says, *"And if the Spirit of Him who raised Jesus from the dead is living in you, He who raised Christ from the dead will also give life to your mortal bodies through His Spirit, who lives in you."*

When God commands Christians into right living, He is only telling Christians to live the way He has re-created them in Christ and empowered them to do so through the indwelling Holy Spirit. Living out a given righteousness through the power of the Holy Spirit is the command, not seeking to earn, or retain, a right standing before God through the Christians' own strength, effort and obedience. Through inner, God-given righteousness to outward right living is the sequence under the New Covenant. The Holy Spirit is the One who facilitates the first and empowers the second. None of it is the work or responsibility of Christians.

The Christian inheritance

Galatians 3:15-18 establishes the position and, therefore, the inheritance of the Christian. When these verses are understood the question of the Christian's position before God, and how that position is achieved, is settled forever. Such understanding brings peace to the striving Christian, hope to the struggling Christian, joy to the "failing" Christian and, beyond the individual, will bring unity within the Church.

Galatians 3:15-18 says, *"Brothers, let me take an example from everyday life. Just as no one can set aside or add to a human covenant which has been duly established, so it is in this case. The promises were spoken to Abraham and to his seed. The Scripture does not say, 'and to seeds,' meaning many people, but 'and to your seed' meaning one person, who is Christ. What I mean is this: The Law, introduced 430 years later, does not set aside the covenant previously established and thus do away with the promise. For if the inheritance depends upon The Law, then it no longer depends on a promise; but God in His grace gave it to Abraham through a promise."*

These verses start by pointing out that no one can add to, take away from, or set aside a duly established covenant. The whole point of a covenant was that it could not be altered in any way. These verses go on to say that God established such an unalterable Covenant with Abraham - and with Abraham's seed. The basis of that relationship was a righteousness given in response to faith. The heir of this Covenant was not Abraham's natural descendants; it was not Israel but was one person - Jesus Christ.

Galatians 3:29 then provides the link between the Abrahamic Covenant and the Christian. Galatians 3:29 says, *"If you belong to Christ, then you are Abraham's seed, and heirs according to the promise."* The Covenant was with Abraham; it was a covenant of faith; Christ was the sole heir to Abraham and the promise. The Christian - belonging to Christ - inherits all that is Christ's and, therefore, becomes heir to the Abrahamic covenant of faith. This is the sequence by which Christians achieve their standing before God - their righteousness given by God in response to faith.

The question may arise, "If the Christian is heir to Abraham, what was the need for Christ?" Firstly, the Abrahamic Covenant was made with only two people - Abraham and Jesus. The Christian, therefore, cannot relate to God directly through Abraham. Christ's sacrifice was necessary in order that the Christian, through faith in the shed blood, might be deemed by God to be *"...in Christ"* (Eph 1:13) and, therefore, an heir to the Abrahamic Covenant (Gal 3:29). This is by no means a technical, theological point. Once understood, this will put an end to so much striving, so much doubt, so much confusion about a Christian's standing before, and, therefore, relationship with God. It is a foundation of the Christian faith. Secondly, Jesus Christ had to come and suffer in order that God's perfect justice may be satisfied. Although Abraham was given righteousness before God as a result of his faith, nevertheless someone still had to die for Abraham's sins - and the sins of those who would inherit through Abraham. Thus, the Christian is heir to two Covenants - that of Abraham and the New Covenant of Christ.

Galatians 3:17 goes on to address the issue of the Law of Moses - a subject which, particularly with the Ten Commandments, causes much confusion and consternation within Christian circles. Should Christians obey it? What is the effect on the Christian's relationship with God if the Christian does not seek to obey the Ten Commandments? Paul answers those questions, and many others, when he writes in Galatians 3:17, *"What I mean is this: the Law, introduced 430 years later, does not set aside the covenant previously established by God and thus do away with the promise."* God, through Paul, is reassuring His people (all Believers in Christ) that the Law of Moses is a matter of total irrelevance to the Christian. In Romans 9:4, it says that the Law was given to Israel. Galatians 3:15 has shown the impossibility of adding to a covenant. Gentile Christians are not Israel and the Law was not given to Gentiles - and that covenant cannot be altered. The Christian relates to God, as explained, through Christ and Abraham - and the separate Covenant of Moses has no bearing on the previously established covenant. When the Christian understands their inheritance, and how they come into that inheritance, it will be seen that, in keeping with everything to do with the Covenant of Christ, it at no stage points the Christian to themself or their effort. The Gospel is all about what God has done, is doing, and will do for humanity.

These few verses in Galatians establish clearly that the inheritance received by the Christian is righteousness from God, and before God, through faith. It is because of this God-given righteousness that Christians enter an eternal relationship with God which begins at conversion and remains uninterrupted for all eternity.

New Covenant righteousness illustrated

The word for "righteousness" in the New Covenant has two applications - one to character, the other to actions. These applications correspond to the inner, eternal righteousness of faith and external right living. Understanding the given, inner righteousness (character) that the Christian always has through faith will prevent the misapplication of individual Scriptures referring to righteousness in the New Testament.

The parable of the Pharisee and the tax collector (Luke 18:9-14) was told by Jesus to those *"…who were confident of their own righteousness* (external right living) *and looked down on everyone else."* There are two important issues addressed in the reason for the telling of this parable. The first is that Jesus is making the point that no one should ever feel confident of their self-righteousness and, secondly, that such self-confidence brings disunity - those who think they are doing well look down on others.

On the face of it, the Pharisees had reasons to be self-confident. The Law demanded that a person fast once a week; this Pharisee fasted twice a week. The Law demanded a tithe of a tenth of all agricultural produce, yet this Pharisee gave a tenth of everything he had. Finally, the Pharisee appeared to be giving the credit to God with his opening statement, *"God, I thank You that I am not like other men…."* On the other hand, the tax collector is aware of only two things - his sinfulness and God's mercy. Acknowledging the one and appealing to the other, he says, only *"God have mercy on me a sinner."* Jesus finishes the parable by informing His listeners that it is the tax collector who goes home justified.

He is still a tax collector when he goes home. Nothing in the Scriptures says that his justification involved a change of livelihood. The important thing is that he went home as a justified tax collector. His character, not his lifestyle, was deemed justified (righteous) because of his faith. This is a very important point for all Christians. There are things in the lives of many Christians that, perhaps, should not be there. It could be something as dramatic, as in this parable, as the way the Christian earns their living. Or less obvious matters, such as patterns of thoughts or behaviours. The point here for all Christians is that these matters do not affect their right standing before God. The Christian's right standing before God is due, entirely, to the work that Christ has done on behalf of the Christian and the Christian's faith in that atoning work. Understanding this truth will bring greater unity because it highlights the fact that the standing of each Christian before God is totally dependent upon the efforts of another - Christ. No one, therefore, has any reason to look up to another Christian (in the sense of believing them to be a better Christian) or to look down on another Christian.

Knowing this truth, of righteousness through faith, gives the Christian confidence before God as the Christian comes to God with the eternal, unalterable righteousness achieved for them by Jesus. With this knowledge, there is no need for a see-saw relationship with God, no need for a sense of heaviness, failure or condemnation.

Knowing they are eternally righteous gives the Christian boldness in their relationship with God which will, irrespective of the day's or week's events, allow them to as Hebrews 4:16 says, *"...approach the throne of grace with confidence so that we may receive mercy and find grace to help us in our time of need."*

The Christian is called into holy living. A lack of holy living may affect the Christian's ability to be an effective witness and so hinder the spread of the Gospel. For that, and other reasons, the Christian should always consider their way of life; but the Christian must never allow their way of life to become a barrier between them and God. It is precisely when the Christian's lifestyle is falling short of what is commanded that the Christian is most in need of God's grace and mercy. Which is why Hebrews 4:16 encourages the Christian to, at that very time, draw close with confidence to the throne of

God. Yet, it is at that very time that many Christians – through a lack of understanding of the Bible's teaching on New Covenant righteousness - draw back from God. That is why so many Christians remain immature. Christians tend to cut themselves off from their source of help at the very time when it is most needed. The Christian's right living is affected by their right standing (internal, God-given righteousness) because as the Christian comes into God's presence, with confidence, they receive – according to Hebrews 4:16 - the help needed to bring about the lifestyle change which brings it more into line with the inner righteousness given by Christ - but it works from the inside out.

New Covenant teachings on righteousness

Hebrews 5:13 identifies the root of Christian immaturity as unfamiliarity with the teaching on righteousness. The following are key New Covenant insights on righteousness. To understand these teachings, ensure the correct application of the word "righteousness" is used. Righteousness, in terms of "right standing before God" is by faith, and faith alone.

Rom 1:17, *"For in the Gospel a righteousness from God is revealed, a righteousness that is by faith from first to last."* Two very important truths about righteousness are revealed in this Scripture. First, the Christian's righteousness is *FROM* God. It flows from heaven to earth, from God to the individual recipient. Secondly, it is a righteousness that comes through faith - entirely, completely by faith.

Romans 3:21 reinforces the point of the God-given nature of righteousness when it says, *"But now a righteousness FROM God, apart from the Law, has been made known...."* Christian righteousness is a gift from God and is unrelated to the way the Christian is living.

Romans 3:22 tells why this righteousness from God is given to the Christian. The verse says, *"This righteousness from God comes through faith in Jesus Christ to all who believe."* The righteousness that God gives is given as a response to faith in Jesus Christ and it is given to all who believe. So, the struggling Christian, who may appear to be failing utterly to live the Christian life, is given the same right standing before God as the Christian who is living a much more obviously Christian life because faith and not lifestyle is the issue. God is the originator of Christian righteousness, and the Christian's faith is the vehicle which allows God to bestow that righteousness upon the individual.

Romans 4:5 again makes the point that it is the Christian's faith which gives them right standing before God; it says, *"However, to the man who does not work but trusts God who justifies the wicked, his faith is credited as righteousness."* As in the case of the tax collector in Luke 18, it is massively reassuring to read that God justifies the wicked. The Good News is that such a truth, far from leading the Christian to abuse God's grace, is more likely to make the Christian love such a gracious God and, as Jesus promised His followers, *"If anyone loves Me, he will obey My teaching"* (John 14:23). So, faith, not works, leads to righteousness.

Romans 4:13 links the righteousness given to Abraham, because of his faith, and that inherited by his heir - which, as has already been explained, means Jesus and then, the Christian.

Romans 5:17 is one of those verses which, once seen and understood, can radically alter the Christian's relationship with God. It says, *"...how much more will those who receive God's abundant provision of grace and of the GIFT of righteousness reign in life through the one man, Jesus Christ."* Righteousness is a GIFT! It is not earned, it is not contributed towards, it is not at risk of being taken away - it is a gift which, once given, belongs to the person receiving it. It is, as is any gift, free. The Christian's part in righteousness is not in striving, continual recommitment, and greater effort; it is simply to receive righteousness as a gift from God. Understanding this one Scripture opens the way to relieving the Christian of any sense of heaviness, striving, failure and so on. It opens the way for the Christian to live in the joy of their salvation, and secure in their eternal standing before God. This verse has enormous implications for Christians. It says that if righteousness and grace are freely received, then, Christians will *"...reign in life."* Once again: great news for the struggling Christian. Great news for the Christian who thinks that God could never be pleased with them, for the Christian who thinks they will never overcome that old sinful pattern of thought or behaviour.

Romans 6:13 commands Christians to *"...not offer the parts of your body to sin".* It goes on: *"...offer the parts of your body to Him as instruments of righteousness."* This refers to a righteousness of behaviour rather than of character and thus does not alter the Christian's standing before God. However, such a command can heavily burden a Christian who may be offering the parts of their body to sin, particularly if that Christian cannot see a way whereby they can stop offering the parts of their body to sin and, so, be obedient to God in this command. This, though, is a verse for the saved, not for the unsaved. Paul confirms this in the following verse, Romans 6:14 when he goes on to say to his readers, *"...you are not under Law, but under grace."* Such a statement can only be said of the saved and sealed Christian. When reading such a verse, and to avoid the burden of failure and condemnation, the Christian must go back to Romans 5:17 and see the way by which they may overcome any sinful habits - by receiving grace and the gift of righteousness. A Christian who struggles with obeying Romans 6:13 should re-read Romans 6:14 and receive the confirmation that *"Sin shall not be your master...because you are under grace."* The Christian, with a full understanding of grace and righteousness, need never fear the commands of God; but, from the Word of God, receive the hope that comes when the way of obedience is rightly grasped.

Romans 6:16 speaks of *"...obedience, which leads to righteousness."* This is the sort of verse that leads many Christians, and unbelievers, to say that a Christian must be obedient to become righteous. Such an understanding flies in the face of so many other Scriptures which speak of Christ as the righteousness of the Christian, of a righteousness that comes from God, of a righteousness which is by faith from beginning to end, and of a righteousness which is a gift from God. The Christian is called, indeed commanded, into obedience; but not the shallow obedience which leads merely to an external righteousness - that is, a show of right living. Christians are called *"...to the obedience that comes from faith"* (Romans 1:5). Such obedience will lead to a fulfilling of God's requirement of the Christian. Jesus was asked, John 6:28, *"What must we do to do the work God requires?"* Jesus answered them, John 6:29, *"The work of God is this: to believe in the One He has sent."* Belief in Jesus Christ meets God's requirement of humanity, according to Jesus Himself, not an endless round of striving for external obedience to a set of rules and regulations.

Romans 8:10 shows the clear distinction between the external battle with sin and the internal, undisturbed righteousness of the Christian. The verse says, *"But if Christ is in you, your body is dead because of sin, yet your spirit is alive because of righteousness."* Christ is in every Christian so this verse, addressed to those who have Christ in them, is addressed to Christians. It is the spirit of the Christian that is righteous and alive, eternally, in and with Christ. The physical body, even of the Christian, is dead because of sin. No Christian should allow the daily activities of their body to separate them from spirit-strengthening communion with their Father. That communion is the Christian's right through faith (John 1:12); it is not earned because of lifestyle, so it is unaffected by daily living.

Romans 9:30-32 are important verses that teach the way of righteousness. Paul writes, *"What then shall we say? That the Gentiles, who did not pursue righteousness, have obtained it, a righteousness that is by faith; but Israel, who pursued a law of righteousness, has not attained it. Why not? Because they pursued it not by faith but as if it were by works."* It could not be more clearly stated. Christians are righteous by faith, and not by works.

The unfortunate reality today is that many Christians are still being taught that a Christian must work for their righteousness – either to gain it, retain it or contribute towards it. The only way to be righteous before God is to believe in Jesus Christ and to receive, as a gift: righteousness from God. If Christians understood this, it would make the Christians the bearers of truly Good News. Good News that would strengthen and encourage many a struggling Christian. Good News that would allow the wayward non-believer to dare to believe that God will accept, and love, even them. Good News that would increase the unity of Christians and, so, increase the effectiveness of Christian witness in the world. It should never be underestimated just how important is a correct understanding of righteousness.

Romans 10:3 shows the danger of seeking to establish one's own righteousness - it can lead to a rejection of God's righteousness. *"Since they* (Israel) *did not know the righteousness that comes from God and sought to establish their own, they did not submit to God's righteousness."* The following verse of **Romans 10:4**, states once again that *"...there may be righteousness for everyone who believes."*

1 Corinthians 1:30 is a glorious verse which shows just how much Christian salvation, and righteousness, is a work of God for man. It starts by stating, *"It is because of Him that you are in Christ Jesus..."* Here is the Word of God declaring very simply that it is God's work that has brought the Christian into the position of being *"...in Christ."* The verse goes on to say, *"...you are in Christ Jesus, who has become for us wisdom from God - that is, our righteousness, holiness, and redemption."* The wonderful news of the Gospel is that Christ Himself is the Christian's righteousness. It is Christ Himself who ensures the Christian's right standing before God, eternally. Jesus cannot be anything less than perfectly righteous and, so, because He is the righteousness of the Christian it means the Christian, likewise, can never be anything less than perfectly righteous in the sight of God. Such knowledge takes the burden of struggling away from the Christian. It allows the Christian to live in *"...the joy of his salvation."* It empowers the Christian to be a channel of encouragement. It also, according to Romans 5:17, will lead the Christian to *"...reign in life."*

Paul writes, in **Galatians 2:21**, *"I do not set aside the grace of God, for if righteousness could be gained through The Law, Christ died for nothing."* God-given righteousness is an outworking of God's grace. Grace, in all its aspects, must be free and unconditional - that is what makes it grace. Righteousness before God, therefore, must be free and unconditional. It is foolishness to think that a Christian's daily living can add to, or take away from, the God-given gift of righteousness - which is Jesus Christ Himself. Every Christian should rejoice in their God-given righteousness and give thanks and glory to God for such a wonderful gift. the focus must remain on what God has done for them, rather than on what they should be doing for God. That is the direction of Scripture.

In **Philippians 3:9** Paul states that he wants to *"...be found in Him (Jesus), not having a righteousness of my own that comes from The Law, but that which is through faith in Christ - the righteousness which comes from God and is by faith."* Paul had earlier declared, in Philippians 3:6, that with regard to *"...legalistic righteousness,"* he was *"...faultless."* So, Paul was not a man who was seeking an easy option to avoid the need for obedience. Paul excelled in his observance of the Law of Moses; but he came to realise that despite all his efforts to live right, he had not achieved right-standing with God. Paul came to understand that such a right-standing must be a gift from God, through Jesus.

There are Scriptures which appear to encourage Christians to strive for their own righteousness. Paul writes to Timothy 1 Timothy 6:11, *"But you, man of God, flee from all this, and pursue righteousness..."* Christians need not be afraid of, or confused by such Scriptures. As was written earlier, there are two applications of the word righteous in the New Testament - one referring to character and the other referring to actions. Righteousness of character, as so many Scriptures have shown, is a gift from God which comes through faith.

Clearly, Paul is not encouraging Timothy to pursue righteousness of character - indeed, he refers to Timothy, in the same verse, as a *"...man of God."* Paul, in this and other such Scriptures, is clearly encouraging his young disciples to pursue a righteousness of actions which will demonstrate his righteousness of character. The Scriptures do teach that sin is no longer an issue between God and man; however, the Scriptures do not encourage the Christian to adopt a casual attitude towards sin. In this verse, Paul is simply encouraging Timothy to adopt a firm attitude towards any wrong living in his life. The same understanding applies to 2 Timothy 2:22 where Paul, once again, encourages Timothy to live out his God-given righteousness.

God has made the Christian righteous, so God encourages Christians to live righteously. He is simply calling the Christians to be what God has made them. The problems come when Christians try to be something beyond what God has called them to be. The Christian must live in the freedom they have, must live in the authority they have been given and must pursue right living; but, at no stage, must a Christian allow lifestyle to separate them from fellowship with God.

Conclusion

Right standing before God (righteousness) is by faith. Right living, or lack of right living, does not affect the Christian's right standing.

Understanding the Scriptures' teachings on righteousness will:

(a) bring increased unity within the church - The Pharisees and The Tax Collector,

(b) increase fruit bearing - Col 1:6 and other verses,

(c) bring increased spiritual maturity - Heb 5:13,

(d) bring a boldness and confidence in the Christian's relationship with God - Heb 4:16

(e) put Christ at the very centre of the Christian's relationship with God - Rom 5:1

For the very important reasons just listed, understanding righteousness is vital for the Christian. A lack of understanding will have a crippling effect on the individual Christian and on the Church overall. The Christian's God-given gift of eternal, unalterable, righteousness through Christ is at the very heart of the Christian Gospel - and that's Good News!

Chapter 6

The doctrine of obedience

Modern teaching

Much modern teaching on obedience involves encouragement to comply with the commands of the Scripture. The focus and emphasis of such teaching is the effort being made by the Christian to live an obedient life. Modern Church teaching applies the traditional definition of the word obedience – compliance with a command or instruction.

A common result of such teaching is a sense of failure or inadequacy within a Christian because of their awareness of their failure to comply with Biblical commands and instructions.

Striving, failure, a heavy burden, unhappiness, a seesaw relationship with the Lord, and a lack of assurance of salvation are often the inevitable results of teachings that focus on the Christian and their efforts to "live the life" and be obedient.

To allow for the teaching of the traditional understanding of the word obedience, and to apply that to the Scriptures, the teacher/preacher must believe there are God-ordained limits to the extent to which a Christian may embrace the freedom contained within God's grace. However, any teaching that places a limit on receiving grace is completely contrary to what the Bible teaches.

So, modern teaching – because it teaches the traditional understanding of the word "obedience" – focuses the Christian upon their own effort (and not on Christ's effort on their behalf) and creates divisions between those who believe the cross of Christ is all-sufficient for salvation and those who believe it is the cross plus the Christian's effort. Modern teaching on obedience is often presented as a check on any tendency in Christians to drift into licentious living – thus presenting grace and obedience as if they are in opposition.

When grace and obedience are seen as alternatives, even opposites, the result is that Christians often pull back from fully embracing grace and thereby a Christian is rendered an ineffective witness for the Gospel. The Christian is left unsure of exactly what the Good News that should be proclaimed is. The message becomes a mixture of Good News and not-so-good news, a mix of grace and Law, faith and works, with a resulting intermittent, see-saw relationship with God. It is not uncommon to find Christians living without any real peace in their relationship with God, and even without an absolute assurance of their salvation. All this stems from modern, unbiblical teachings on obedience – due to the traditional use of that word – which has no biblical mandate.

Biblical answers to questions on Christian obedience

Understood properly, the Bible provides clear teachings, as explained below, to questions around the issue of obedience that every Christian needs to be able to confidently answer. They are:

Question 1: Is the Christian under an obligation to be obedient to God?

With one specific exception – which will be explained later in this chapter - the answer to this most fundamental question is, quite simply, "No." There is no doubt or confusion - it is clearly and unarguably, "No."

Many Christians may seriously struggle with such an answer and, primarily out of fear of offending God – perhaps even believing that will jeopardise their salvation – will pull back from daring to embrace this truth. The following explanations will remove any such fear and allow Christians to embrace the revolutionary truth that they are under no obligation to be obedient to God (apart from the one exception). And receiving that revolutionary truth will revolutionise their personal relationship with God.

A. Saved by grace

The New Covenant is a Covenant of grace. All Christians should know Ephesians 2:8-9: *"For it is by grace you have been saved, through faith -and this is not from yourselves, it is the gift of God - not by works, so that no one can boast."*

The first part of understanding what God is looking for in terms of obedience is to understand the word *"saved."* For many, it means they will go to heaven when they leave this planet but it means so much more than just that. To be *"saved"* is to be brought into a relationship with God, in this life, from the moment faith in Christ is realised.

That relationship with God – a sovereign choice of God's and not related in any way to the Christian's lifestyle – is eternal. John 17:2 says, *"For You granted Him authority over all people that He might give eternal life to all those You have given Him."* In the next verse, John 17:3, John then defines "eternal life" saying, John 17:3, *"Now this is eternal life: that they know You, the only true God, and Jesus Christ, whom You have sent."*

So, knowing God, through being in a relationship with Him, through faith in Jesus, is the start of the Christian's eternal life – although, for the technically minded, *"eternal"* cannot have a starting point! However, this conundrum is resolved when Paul explains to Titus in Titus 1:1-3; *"Paul, a servant of God and an apostle of Jesus Christ to further the faith of God's elect and their knowledge of the truth that leads to godliness in <u>the hope of eternal life, which God, who does not lie, promised before the beginning of time,</u> and which now at His appointed season He has brought to light through the preaching entrusted to me by the command of God our Saviour…"*

So, to be saved is to be in a relationship with God, an eternal relationship that began, by God's promise – before time itself, and a relationship that, being eternal, cannot be broken or interrupted.

On this basis, the Christian's obedience to God's commands and instructions- based upon the usual definition of that word (compliance with a command or instruction) – is irrelevant in terms of their relationship with God and their salvation which are, in fact, the same thing.

Accordingly, there can be no obligation to adhere to something that no longer has any relevance – compliance with a set of commands and instructions. Such teaching has been imported from the Old Covenant, the

Law, where compliance was the basis of the Covenant and the basis, therefore, of the Israelite's relationship with God.

B. The nature of grace.

A fundamental truth of grace is that grace, to be grace, must be free. The gift of Jesus, the eternal life that comes through His death and resurrection, and all the blessings poured out on the Christian through Jesus are all outworkings of God's grace, which means that they are all freely given. If a Christian picks up any obligation because of what God has done for them, then God's work on humanity's behalf ceases to be grace and simply becomes an exchange - God's saving work in exchange for, in this case, a person's obedience. A multitude of Scriptures testify that a person is saved by grace and that God's grace is freely given. If these numerous Scriptures are true – which, of course, they are – then, a person can never be placed under _any_ obligation or condition because of what God has done. That lack of obligation must, very obviously, include a lack of obligation to be obedient.

C. The child of God has been set free.

Galatians 5:1 says, _"It is for freedom that Christ has set us free."_ The purpose of Christ setting the Christian free was that the Christian might live in that freedom. In the Scripture, there is no restriction given, in relation to the Christian's standing before God, to what the Bible terms _"...the glorious freedom of the children of God."_ (Rom 8:21). In terms of the Christian's standing before God, they may do what they want, when they want, with whom they want, how they want and where they want. This is the boundless freedom, and unlimited security, which Christ purchased for the Christian at Calvary.

It is the very boundless nature of this freedom that scares Christians into not embracing it. It sounds too much like license. To avoid this supposed license, and due to a lack of understanding of the empowering nature of grace, Christians, individually and as churches and denominations, begin to impose restrictions, limitations and obligations upon Christians. Those impositions then become a burden to many weaker Christians. Yet examination of the Scriptures reveals that those impositions have no Biblical mandate. In fact, the same Scripture, Galatians 5:1, which speaks of the freedom of the Believer in Christ, urges the Christian, _"Stand firm, then, and do not let yourselves be burdened again by a yoke of slavery."_ That "yoke" is the same one which Peter spoke against in Acts 15:10 when he spoke against those who were seeking to compel Gentile Believers to obey the Law of Moses.

Question 2: If there is no obligation to be obedient, is not license the inevitable result of living under grace?

Those who argue that embracing the boundless freedom of Christ will inevitably lead to license may not have weighed the difference between obligation and responsibility. An obligation is compulsory, whereas responsibility, although the best course of action, remains a matter of individual choice. Responsibility fits in with a Gospel of grace, obligation does not.

Paul sets the context within which the many commands for holy living under the New Covenant are given. In 1 Corinthians 6:12, Paul writes, *"Everything is permissible for me, but not everything is beneficial."* This reinforces the concept of the unlimited freedom of Christ. An amazing thing about Christians is that they will proclaim a Scripture, believing with all their heart in the unchallengeable truth of God's holy Word, and then immediately contradict that Scripture if it doesn't "sit right" with their understanding of Christianity.

1 Corinthians 6:12 is a good example of this. Christians will declare, with Paul, that *"Everything is permissible..."* but will then immediately follow that up by listing what - in their confused opinion is, actually, NOT permissible. *"Everything is permissible..."* declares the Bible, "...but you must not have sex before marriage," responds the Christian. *"Everything is permissible..."* proclaims God's Word - "...but you must not get drunk," choruses the Christian. These incorrect impositions of restrictions are made far worse when, as so often happens, it is linked to the Christian's ongoing security in their salvation. The implication is made clear, "If you carry on having sex outside marriage, or getting drunk, (etc.) you may end up losing your salvation."

And so, the confused teaching and understanding goes on. People who believe totally in the Bible as God's inspired and holy Word will not hesitate, due to a lack of understanding of grace, to contradict it when to accept it would appear to be license - as though the Word itself would encourage license! Not only does the concept of grace demand limitless freedom but in

1 Corinthians 6:12, and other places, the Bible spells out clearly that there truly is limitless freedom in Christ.

Having proclaimed the fundamental truth that, in keeping with a Gospel of grace, everything is permissible, Paul then goes on in the same verse to unfold the reasons why recklessly embracing that limitless freedom may not be beneficial. There are three reasons that Paul gives as justification for a self-imposed restriction on the way Christians live.

The first is revealed in the second part of 1 Corinthians 6:12. The verse continues, *"Everything is permissible for me - but I will not be mastered by anything."* Paul chooses not to exercise the complete freedom that he has in Christ because he, Paul, does not want to be mastered by anything. It is wise for Christians to <u>choose</u> to limit the freedom that God gives them, but the limitation is a choice by the Christian for the benefit of the Christian and other people. Any such limitation in no way enhances the Christian's standing before God or contributes to the assurance of their salvation. Similarly, any lack of such limitation in no way detracts from the Christian's standing before God or places in jeopardy the assurance of their salvation.

If a Christian has a sinful habit in which they indulge - safe in the knowledge that all sin is paid for - that habit will soon become one which has an irresistible power and the Christian, through ignoring God's Word, may find themself *"mastered"* by that habit. Paul points out in this verse that it is not of benefit to the individual Christian to engage in limitless freedom to the extent that they end up losing some of that freedom. However, there is no obligation imposed through this verse. The Christian is advised of the wisest course of action and then left with the freedom to choose whether to follow that advice. That whole scenario agrees with the Gospel of Grace.

It does not have to be an obviously sinful habit which gains mastery. Limitless freedom includes the freedom to impose restrictions. It could be an often-repeated religious restriction or exercise which eventually detracts from the joy and peace with God which rightfully belong to the Christian and, being thus not beneficial, is an unwise use of the freedom of the Christian.

In 1 Corinthians 8:9, Paul gives the second reason why Christians should willingly choose to put a restriction upon their freedom. The Scripture says, *"Be careful, however, that the exercise of your freedom does not become a stumbling block to the weak.*" Once again, this guidance fits in comfortably with the Gospel of Grace. The guidance is put forward by Paul for the benefit of other people – those not so secure in their Christian knowledge and faith. If the exercise of a sinful habit, or the exercise of a legalistic ritual or restriction, is seen by a weaker Christian, or by a non-Christian, as legitimising such activity, then, it should be given up. The restriction is for the purpose of being a better witness and example. There is no compulsion in this advice. It is the wise thing to do - live in such a way that does not cause a weaker person to stumble - but it is a matter of individual choice as to whether that advice is followed. Equally, there is no suggestion that the following, or failing to follow of this advice will in any way affect the Christian's standing before God.

In 1 Corinthians 10:23, Paul gives the third reason why Christians may choose to voluntarily limit their otherwise unrestricted freedom. Paul writes, *"Everything is permissible but not everything is beneficial. Everything is permissible - but not everything is constructive."*

Within this letter to the Corinthians, Paul writes four times the phrase *"Everything is permissible."* There is such freedom in that truth for any Christian who is struggling with some sinful habit or desire, and such freedom for the non-Christian who holds back from embracing the faith because of activities or thought patterns which they feel will make them unacceptable to God.

In 1 Corinthians 10:23, Paul says that although everything is permissible, not everything is constructive. And in verse 24, he goes on to explain in what way some things are not constructive. He writes, *"Nobody should seek his own good, but the good of others."* An individual Christian's maturity and personal relationship with God may allow that Christian to live in a certain way; but, if another sees that lifestyle and, perhaps by copying it, is harmed by it, then the freedom enjoyed by the stronger Christian is now, in these circumstances, no longer constructive - but potentially destructive. This again, is a choice made by Christians which is in keeping with grace. It is a choice the stronger Christian makes based on helping others, and not on enhancing their standing before God.

Living, therefore, under grace will not lead to license. Of course, there is a Biblically right way to live as a Christian; but it is a matter of choice as to whether the individual Christian lives in that right way. Whether or not a Christian does live "the right way" will not affect the Christian's standing before God - although recklessly embracing freedom may lead to a loss of freedom (being "mastered" by something) and to being a poor witness who causes others to stumble.

If a Christian is living according to the Bible, that Christian will not end up with a set of rules and regulations of what they can and cannot do, but that Christian will receive guidance on why their freedom should, on occasion, be voluntarily curtailed.

That might almost sound like splitting hairs - to say, when the result is the same, that a Christian is choosing to be obedient to God's Word rather than being compelled to obey, but it is a most fundamental difference. It is the difference between grace and Law. It is a difference that brings freedom, peace, and joy to any Christian striving to obey. It is a difference that removes all pressure from the Christian. This, in turn, deepens the love the Christian has for God - a God who is now making no demands but is truly accepting that Christian exactly as they are. As the love a Christian has for God deepens, amazing things begin to happen. Jesus Christ said, *"If you love Me, you will obey what I command"* (John 14:15). The sequence is to love God first, then - and the Christian has Christ's promise on the matter - the obedience will follow as the Christian chooses, out of love for Christ, to follow the Biblical advice and example of Jesus, therein. Christians today must get that sequence in the right order and must work on deepening their love for Christ.

Question 3: To what then should the Christian choose to be obedient?

Having established that there is no obligation to be obedient, but that a Christian, nevertheless, has a responsibility to live in a certain way, the question arises: "To what then should the Christian choose to be obedient?"

The first thing to recognise is that there are two areas within which Christian obedience applies. It is vitally important to recognise these two areas and to put them in the correct order of priority. The areas are: (1) spiritual obedience and (2) practical obedience. The tendency in much modern teaching is to emphasise practical obedience without teaching that this can only meaningfully occur following spiritual obedience.

A. Spiritual obedience

In John 6:28, Jesus was asked, *"What do we have to do to do the works God requires?"* The answer given by Jesus in the subsequent verse gives only one *"work"* that is required by God. Jesus said, in John 6:29, *"The work of God is this: to believe in the One He has sent."* They came looking for a list - *"the works"* God requires; Jesus gave them one task, to believe. John emphasises this point in 1 John 3:23. He writes, *"And this is His command: to believe in the name of His Son, Jesus Christ, and to love one another as He commanded us."* This is the priority and the sequence - faith, and then the outworking of that faith.

It might appear that there is a conflict here with grace because there is now an obligation - an obligation to have faith. However, this does not create conflict within a Gospel of Grace - which cannot, by definition, impose any obligation - because in Ephesians 2:8, it is written that God Himself gives the Christian the faith needed for salvation. So, yes, faith is a requirement; but, in keeping with grace, God meets that requirement for the Christian: *"For it is by grace you have been saved, through faith - and this not from yourselves, it is the gift of God..."* Eph 2:8.

In the first area of spiritual obedience, the requirement is, "Have faith." As God gives the Christian the faith that God requires then every Christian is, obviously, obedient to the fundamental requirement of God as expressed by His Son in John 6:29.

An examination of the Scriptures shows just how much that God-given faith achieves for the Christian. Acts 26:18 says the Christian is sanctified by faith, Romans 1:17 (also: Rom 3:22, Rom 4:5, Rom 9:30) says that a Christian is made righteous through faith and Romans 5:1 says the Christian is justified through faith. Faith saves, justifies, counts as righteousness, and sanctifies the Christian. Faith is God-given. Having given the Christian faith, God then counts that faith as obedience.

The Scriptures reinforce the truth that having faith and being obedient are the same thing by showing that God counts lack of faith as disobedience. In John 3:18, when speaking about faith in Jesus, it says, *"...whoever does not believe stands condemned already because he has not believed...."* Lack of faith in Jesus is given as the only reason for condemnation under the New Covenant. In Romans 9:32, Paul writes that Israel failed to achieve righteousness because *"...they pursued it not by faith but as if it were by works."* Romans 14:23 puts it very simply that, *"...everything that does not come from faith is sin."* In Hebrews 3:18-19, the writer is addressing the issue of faith and obedience. The writer asks the question, *"And to whom did God swear that they would never enter His rest if not to*

those who disobeyed? So, we see that they were not able to enter, because of their unbelief."
These verses clearly link disobedience and disbelief.

So, the primary requirement of God, in terms of obedience, is the spiritual obedience of faith in Christ. If a person has faith, which is given by God, then God counts that person as saved, justified, righteous and sanctified and therefore able to enjoy a daily relationship with God, not marred in any way by the person's day-to-day lifestyle.

B. Practical obedience

The Scriptures provide a mass of evidence that a Christian is not under the Law of Moses. It is sufficient here to quote just two Scriptures to briefly make the point. In Acts 15, Peter addresses the issue of whether Gentile Believers should be required to be circumcised and obey the Law of Moses. In verses 9-11, Peter says, *"He* (God) *made no distinction between us and them* (the Gentiles), *for He purified their hearts by faith. Now then, why do you try to test God by putting on the necks of the disciples a yoke* (the Law) *that neither we nor our fathers have been able to bear? No! We believe it is through the grace of our Lord Jesus that we are saved, just as they are."* Peter clearly rebukes those who would put Christians under The Law of Moses.

Hebrews 7:12 explains with great and simple clarity why the Christian is not under the Old Covenant (the Law of Moses). It says, *"For when there is a change of the priesthood, there must also be a change of the law."* With Christ, the priesthood changed. No longer do Aaron and his descendants fulfil the role of High Priest of Israel - although Israel itself did not understand this truth - for now, as Hebrews 3:1 and other Scriptures make clear, Jesus Christ is the eternal High Priest for all Christians.

Paul gives a title to the new law which started with the new priesthood. In 1 Corinthians 9:20-21, he writes: *"To those under the Law I became like one under the Law (though I myself am not under the Law), so as to win those under the Law. To those not having the Law I became like one not having the Law (though I am not free from God's law but am under Christ's Law) ..."* This then is the name of the Rule of Life, or Law, which applies to a Christian. A Christian is not obliged to obey it because it is a Law introduced in the Dispensation of grace, but it is beneficial for the Christian, and others if they do.

The nature of Christ's law

Paul wrote in 1 Corinthians 6:12, *"Everything is permissible for me - but I will not be mastered by anything."* The paradox of obeying Christ's Law and self-limiting personal freedom is that it safeguards greater freedom. Willingly surrendering some freedom ensures there is no loss of freedom to some enslaving habit. This truth about Christ's Law is testified to in James 1:25 where he writes, *"But the man who looks intently into the perfect law that gives freedom...."* A law which gives freedom! Not the heavy yoke that Israel was unable to bear. Not the Law by which *"...we were held prisoners..."* (Galatians 3:23). A Christian should choose to be obedient to a law, or rule of life, which enhances and strengthens their freedom. That fits in with the Gospel of grace and with the mission of Christ - as that is expressed in Galatians 5:1. It will help a Christian determine which law they are following if they ask themself the question: "Is this law, this rule of life, under which I am living the liberating law of Christ or the heavy yoke of the enslaving Law of the Old Covenant of Moses?"

Christ's law is a law of love.

In 1 Corinthians 16:14, Paul directs the Christian, *"Do everything in love."* That is the reason for a Christian living by Christ's law - that love may be pre-eminent. This again provides a useful indicator of which law, and therefore which Covenant, the Christian is living under. Is love the motivation for what the Christian is, or is not doing? Or are fear and obligation the motivators – in which case that Christian is not living under Christ's law?

Christ's law is a law which is concerned first and foremost with the serving of others.

In Galatians 6:2, Paul directs the Christian to, *"Carry each other's burdens...."* and goes on to say, *"...and in this way you will fulfill the law of Christ."* This fits in completely with the mission and example of Jesus and is another guide as to which law the Christian is following.

None of the revealed purposes of Christ's law is to enhance the standing of the Christian before God; they are all to do with bettering the lot of the Christian's fellow men and women. Christ Himself testified that, *"By this all men will know you are My disciples, if you love one another"* (John 13:35). Jesus said that *"My yoke is easy and My burden is light"* (Matt 11:30) and John confirms this in 1 John 5:3, when he writes, *"...His commands are not burdensome."*

In summary, that to which a Christian should choose to be obedient is the law of Christ. It is a law which brings freedom, which is motivated by love, which is primarily concerned with the well-being of others and which is not a heavy load. If those conditions are not fulfilled then, no matter what the motivation, any supposed obedience is outside of the law of Christ and, as such, has no Biblical mandate.

Question 4: How can the Christian consistently choose to follow Christ's Law?

So far it has been established that there is no obligation to be practically obedient, but there is a responsibility to live right and that this is achieved by choosing to adhere to the law of Christ.

The next issue for a Christian who wishes to follow their Master is, "How is a Christian expected to be practically obedient?" This is a very important question because if a Christian is simply left with their own strength and good intentions, then, they are in no different a position to the Israelites living under the Covenant of Moses. What is the difference for the Christian? How can the Christian stop the law of Christ becoming a legalistic burden? What hope, and peace, is there for the Christian who seems to be forever failing to live by the law of Christ?

A fundamental truth about the Covenant of Grace, the New Covenant in Christ's blood, is that it is all about what God has done, is doing and will do for man. This includes the area of practical obedience. At no point, under the New Covenant, is the Christian ever called upon to do anything in their own strength. God's equipping of a Christian includes faith, the Holy Spirit, grace, love and, of course, Jesus Himself. Five gifts which God has given to Christians by which they may live out the life to which they have been called.

A. Faith

In Romans 1:5, Paul writes, *"Through Him and for His name's sake we received grace and apostleship to call people from among all the Gentiles to the obedience that comes from faith."* A Christian is called to an obedience that springs from faith. This is not the obedience of striving and never-ending resolutions to do better. This is not the obedience of trying to be someone or something which, in reality, has not yet been achieved. A Christian is called to a practical obedience that says, "I can - because God says I can." If that kind of faith is not present for any given issue, then all that is left is striving. That striving, because it is not empowered by God-given faith, is a complete waste of time - as many a frustrated and despondent Christian will testify. There are many Scriptures which make this point: 1 Corinthians 16:13, *"...stand firm in the faith"*; 2 Corinthians 1:24, *"It is by faith you stand firm."* 1 Thessalonians 1:3 speaks of *"...your work produced by faith."* Everywhere the emphasis is on what a Christian will achieve practically through faith. That includes the ability to be practically obedient. That faith is a gift from God so, in keeping with the Covenant of Grace, Christian practical obedience becomes God's responsibility. That takes all the pressure off a Christian and opens a Christian up to being more practically obedient.

B. The Holy Spirit

Salvation is a gift of God which contains many aspects. For some Christians, salvation means that they will not go to hell when they die, yet salvation means so much more. Amongst other things, salvation means a daily relationship with God in this life. That is brought about through the gift of the Holy Spirit. A Christian will become practically obedient to the law of Christ because they have the indwelling Holy Spirit, one of whose tasks is to bring about that practical obedience. Romans 15:16 speaks of the fact that the Gentile Believers have become acceptable to God, having been *"...sanctified by the Holy Spirit."* It is the Spirit's job to bring about the sanctification of a Christian. That is Good News! No more striving; no more sense of failure, and of letting God down. Now a Christian's sanctification is God's responsibility. Philippians 2:13 states that, *"...it is God who works in you to will and act according to His good purpose."* Once again, the Scriptures teach that God places no burden upon a Christian but, instead, accepts Himself the responsibility for making the Christian acceptable to Himself. Another task of the Holy Spirit, according to Jesus, is to lead the Christian into a knowledge of all truth (John 16:13). Part of the truth the Spirit will reveal is that the Christian is not under the Law of the Old Covenant. The Scriptures say that *"...the power of sin is the Law."* (1 Corinthians 15:56). If a Christian is freed from the power of the Law, then that Christian is freed from the power of sin. That is the Word of God, and the Spirit will guide the Christian into that truth. The Law of the Old Covenant does not have the power to <u>make</u> the Christian sin but the Law has the power – through a sense of guilt and failure - to make the Christian feel unworthy of communion with God and to, therefore, withdraw from that communion; although it is the very source of their strength and help when unholy living persists in the life of a Christian. The Spirit will encourage life-giving fellowship between the Christian and God by showing that the Christian is always acceptable to God, because of Jesus.

C. Grace

Many Christians think of grace as an easy option, and an alternative to practical obedience. The Scriptures make it clear that the opposite is true, in that grace is the very source of a Christian's practical obedience. Romans 5:17 says in the second half of the verse, *"...how much more will those who receive God's abundant provision of grace and of the gift of righteousness reign in life through the one man, Jesus Christ."* This Scripture makes it very clear that it is the receiving of grace which allows the Christian to reign in life. It is not by striving that greater victories will come, it is by receiving grace. That goes against human wisdom - how can more be achieved by making less effort? Christians are not encouraged to make less effort. God simply directs them to where their effort should go. Christians should put their effort into receiving grace, and the gift of God-given righteousness, and through that they will reign in life. Romans 5:2 speaks of *"...this grace in which we now stand."* It is by grace the Christian will stand. That grace is entered into, as Romans 5:2 also states, not by striving but *"...by faith."* Grace is the source of hard work in the life of a Christian - as both 1 Corinthians 15:10 and 2 Corinthians 9:8 make it clear. Grace, then, is another provision which God has made by which the Christian will be enabled to live out the Christian life.

D. Love

Love is the law under which the Christian lives. Love is the command of Jesus Christ - John 15:12, and elsewhere. Love is the source of practical obedience in the life of a Christian. In John 14:15, Jesus says, *"If you love Me, you will obey what I command."* Once again, God is re-directing the effort of the well-meaning Christian. It is not striving against sinful habits and passions that will get the Christian very far, it is deepening their love of Jesus that makes the difference. That is the Word of God - and that is Good News! The sequence is love, then practical obedience. Even this love, God has provided for the Christian. Romans 5:5 says that *"...God has poured out His love into our hearts by the Holy Spirit whom He has given us."* This is all entirely in keeping with the New Covenant which is all about God's provision for humanity. At no point in the Scripture's teachings on practical obedience under the New Covenant, does God point the Christian to themself and their own effort. Jesus says, "love Me and you will obey Me" and then God gives Christians His love in their hearts. In 1 Thessalonians 1:3, Paul commends the church there for: *"...your labour prompted by love..."* The Bible says that *"God is love"* (1 John 4:16). Love is the most powerful motivating force known to humanity. Love is the source of Christian practical obedience. Any other motivation is doomed to be short-lived and to end in failure. Christians should receive the love God has for them, the love God has given them, and allow that love to flow through their life in acts of practical obedience - which, in accordance with the law of Christ, will primarily manifest as acts of caring for others.

E. Jesus Christ

Responsibility for a Christian's practical obedience falls squarely onto the shoulders of the Lord Jesus Christ. In Romans 14:4, Paul asks the question, *"Who are you to judge someone else's servant? To his own master he stands or falls. And he will stand, for the Lord is able to make him stand."* There is the promise of Holy Scripture that despite any supposed shortcomings, weaknesses, sinful habits and so on that may be in a Christian's life, the Christian will stand - because Jesus Himself will make that Christian stand. The joyful news is that the responsibility for the spiritual security of every Christian rests not with a Christian but with the Son of God. And that's very Good News! Philippians 4:13 points to Jesus as the source of Christian strength: *"I can do everything through Him who gives me strength"* and 1 Timothy 1:12 says, *"I thank Christ Jesus our Lord, who has given me strength...."* It is Christ's task to ensure the security of each Christian and to empower them to live the life to which the Christian is called.

Question 5: What are the consequences if a Christian is not practically obedient?

The most important point to remember is that faith in Jesus Christ – and such faith is God-given – is regarded as obedience under the New Covenant. Accordingly, as long as faith in Christ remains – and it is the Holy Spirit's responsibility to ensure it does remain – then, a Christian is regarded as living in the obedience God requires of them.

Therefore, the discussion in response to the question, *"What are the consequences if a Christian is not obedient?"* relates to the lifestyle of a Christian, which has no bearing upon their salvation nor upon their day-to-day relationship with the Lord.

Under the Old Covenant, the punishment for disobedience was clearly spelt out in Deuteronomy 28. God effectively told Israel, "If you obey Me, I will bless you; if you disobey Me, I will curse every aspect of your personal, communal and national life." What is referred to in that chapter is the practical obedience through lifestyle, because that was the basis of the Old Covenant. Obedience to the Law of Moses was the Old Covenant requirement, and the Israelite system of religious sacrifices was the requirement for any failures in obedience. These failures did impact on the day-to-day distant relationship between an Israelite and God but they could be compensated for, and the relationship restored, following the religious sacrifice.

Many Christians, through lack of understanding of the Scriptures, live with the same Old Covenant fear of God's displeasure if they fail to live according to the call upon their life to, *"...be holy as I am holy"*: 1 Peter 1:15, and elsewhere.

These failures to, *"...be holy..."* relate to the day-to-day practical outworking of a Christian's faith. But, as long as faith remains, a Christian is being obedient and completing the work that Jesus spelt out in John 6:29: *"This is the work of God, that you believe in Him whom He sent."*

It may be that the Christan incurs some adverse result from their practical disobedience, or it may be that another person incurs some adverse result or hardship as a result of a Christian's practical disobedience, but in terms of the practically disobedient Christian's relationship with and standing before God, there is no consequence at all.

So, the Biblically correct answer to the question, *"What are the consequences if a Christian is not obedient"* is that a Christian – as someone who believes in Christ – cannot, in the eyes of God and according to the Scriptures, be disobedient. It is only the non-believers who are disobedient in the eyes of God and that is only because of their lack of faith in Christ.

In Romans 8:1, there is a well-known verse which is so often quoted by Christians yet equally so often set aside in their relationship with God when the Christian becomes especially aware of sin in their life. The verse says, *"Therefore, there is now no condemnation for those who are in Christ Jesus."* The word "No" must mean just that - there is NO condemnation for the Christian. That must obviously include those times when a Christian does not live up to their high calling. It has already been established that the Christian is saved, justified, made righteous and sanctified by faith. It follows then that as long as faith remains, there is nothing in a Christian's lifestyle that can negatively affect the Christian's position or relationship with God.

Conclusion

The Rule of Life for the Christian is Christ's Law. It is a law which brings freedom, is rooted in love, is primarily concerned with the Christian's serving of others and is not a heavy load.

The obedience required by God is that a person should believe in His Son Jesus Christ. Practical obedience to Christ's Law then flows from this spiritual obedience.

Grace is not grace if it carries obligations, strings or conditions; therefore, practical obedience to Christ's Law cannot be an obligation under the New Covenant.

Practical obedience to Christ's Law is a responsibility which is of benefit to the Christian and other people, but in no way enhances or detracts from the Christian's relationship with God.

The Christian is empowered to choose to be practically obedient to Christ's Law by the God-given gifts of faith, the Holy Spirit, grace, love and Jesus Christ. The Christian is never expected to be obedient – spiritually or practically - in their own strength.

"By the grace of God I am what I am, and His grace to me was not without effect. No I worked harder than all of them - yet not I, but the grace of God that was with me": 1 Corinthians 15:10.

Chapter 7

The doctrine of sin

What is sin?

Having explained the New Testament doctrines of repentance, forgiveness, righteousness and obedience, and seen how in each case the responsibility for meeting God's requirement in each area is taken on by God, and not left for Christians to achieve or satisfy the requirements within each case, the understanding of where sin sits within the New Covenant must now be addressed.

The Bible gives a clear and simple definition of sin. It says in Romans 14:23 that, *"...everything that does not come from faith is sin."* In that verse is a glimpse of human sinfulness. Everything said, done or even thought that is not rooted in faith in Jesus Christ, and the written Word of God, is sin. Every worry, every fear, every doubt – whatever is not of faith is sin.

In 1 John 3:4, it says, *"Everyone who sins breaks the law; in fact, sin is lawlessness."* Paul, in 1 Corinthians 9 writes about his move from the Law of Moses to the Law of Christ. In verse 21, he writes, *"...I am not free from God's law but am under Christ's law."* Christ's Law can be summed up by two Scriptures. The first is John 15:12, which says, *"My command is this: Love each other as I have loved you."* The second is Galatians 6:2, which says, *"Carry each other's burdens, and in this way you will fulfill the law of Christ."* So, every thought, word or deed that is not rooted in sacrificial, agape love is a sin. Every thought, word or deed that does not seek to lessen the burden of others is a sin. If Christians are not loving and serving others all the time, as Jesus did, they are living for self. It will always be either "others" or "self."

As Christians begin to understand these Scriptures, they not only answer the question, "What is sin?" but they begin to glimpse the extent of their own sinfulness. But even as they glimpse their sinfulness, they can see hope rather than despair. The extent to which Christians sin, once they understand their sinfulness, highlights the foolishness of thinking that they are responsible for maintaining their relationship with God through striving towards right living and/or through continual repentance and requests for forgiveness.

Christian Attitudes to sin

The issue for Christians is not whether they sin, but what is their attitude to those sins. For example, there are those who would argue that sins can still act as a barrier between the Christian and God. Yet, such a position is to deny, or at least not understand, the achievement of the cross and the many truths of Scripture that declare that, *"Christ died for our sins."*

Some will argue that having been saved by the blood of Christ, it is then the Christian's responsibility to maintain their relationship with God - either through the way they live or, in the event of their sinning, through repeated "repentance" and asking for forgiveness. Such a position denies the sufficiency of the cross and, also, shows little awareness of the utterly fallen state of humanity and the woefully sinful state of every Christian.

Then, some would seek to make a difference between so-called intentional sin and unintentional sin. But the Scriptures teach that God requires a sacrifice for every sin. The books of Leviticus and Numbers reveal God's perspective on unintentional sin, including offenses committed unknowingly Although Christians are not under the Law of Moses, God's attitude to sin, and His requirement for a sacrifice for every sin, has not changed. Additionally, 1 Corinthians 10:13 says, *"No temptation has seized you except what is common to man. And God is faithful; He will not let you be tempted beyond what you can bear. But when you are tempted, He will also provide a way out so that you can stand up under it."* So, under the New Covenant, there is absolutely no excuse for any sin because, the Bible says, for every temptation, it is within the Christian's capability to resist it – through a God-given way out.

So, does a Christian sin?

There is only one Biblically correct answer to the question, "Does a Christian sin?" The answer, though, comes in two parts. Firstly, **a Christian cannot sin in the sight of God**; secondly, **a Christian can do nothing but sin in their own eyes.**

Those Christians who still feel burdened by their sin, or who spend a lot of time trying to overcome their sin (when that effort could go into serving others) and, indeed, all Christians – must learn to separate the way they see themselves from the way God sees them, and nowhere is this more important than in the issue of sin.

PART ONE:
A Christian cannot sin in the sight of God

A look through some New Testament Scriptures will reveal how God sees the Christian and why He sees them in this way.

Romans 3:21-24: *"But now a righteousness from God, apart from law, has been made known, to which the Law and the Prophets testify. This righteousness from God comes through faith in Jesus Christ to all who believe. There is no difference, for all have sinned and fall short of the glory of God and are justified freely by His grace through the redemption that came by Christ Jesus."* In the New Covenant, the righteousness that is required for a Christian to be in relationship with God is a righteousness that comes "from" God. In other words, it is God-given. The justification that is given is given "…freely by His grace." So, the Christian's right-standing (righteousness) before God is something that God achieves for the Christian.

Romans 3:28 and Romans 5:1 declare that the Christian is justified through faith. It is not through works, and there is no responsibility upon the Christian to either gain or maintain their relationship with God.

Romans 5:19 provides an understanding of how God can see Christians as righteous – despite the way they may live each day. It says, *"For just as through the disobedience of the one man the many were made sinners, so also through the obedience of the one man the many will be made righteous."* So, it is not the Christian's obedience that contributes in any way to their standing before God, it is the obedience of Jesus Christ. Through His obedience, Christians have been made righteous – that is how God is able to see Christians as righteous.

Romans 6:1-3 says: *"What shall we say, then? Shall we go on sinning so that grace may increase? By no means! We died to sin; how can we live in it any longer? Or don't you know that all of us who were baptised into Christ Jesus were baptised into His death?"* And verses 6-7 say, *"For we know that our old self was crucified with Him so that the body of sin might be done away with, that we should no longer be slaves to sin - because anyone who has died has been freed from sin."*

Christians do not sin in the eyes of God because they have died to sin – not because they make a lot of effort not to sin (and the Bible shows how pointless that effort is). Overcoming sin, as with everything in the New Covenant, is something that is achieved by faith. A Christian's faith allows God to see them as being without sin, and a Christian's faith will give them victory over sin on a day-to-day basis; thus, bringing their personal experience more into line with God's declared view of things.

Romans 8:30 explains very simply that all the works that needed to be done to initiate and maintain a relationship with God, have been done by God Himself. The verse says, *"And those He predestined, He also called; those He called, He also justified; those He justified, He also glorified."* So, from beginning to end – from predestination right through to glorification – everything is a work of God. This allows God to see the Christian as sinless. It is He who does everything, and nothing is left as the responsibility of the Christian.

Another verse that explains how God can see Christians as sinless is 1 Corinthians 1:30. It says: *"It is because of Him (God) that you are in Christ Jesus, who has become for us wisdom from God - that is, our righteousness, holiness and redemption."* The Christian's righteousness, holiness and redemption are not things they achieve or contribute towards. It is Jesus who has become these attributes on behalf of Christians. He is each Christian's righteousness – therefore, Christians are not constantly changing their level of righteousness depending upon how much effort they are making against sin. Jesus Himself is the Christian's holiness, and through Him, they are continually seen as holy in the eyes of God. And Jesus is the Christian's redemption.

What this is saying is also expressed in Galatians 3:27 which says, *"…for all of you who were baptised into Christ have clothed yourselves with Christ."* Romans

6:3 says that when a Christian was baptised into Christ's death, they died to sin, and this verse in Galatians explains how that happens. It is because the Christian becomes, in God's sight, *"...clothed with Christ."* Therefore, He then becomes the Christian's righteousness and holiness. Christians may not understand exactly "how" this happens, but they do know that it does happen because the Bible says so.

Ephesians 1:4 says, *"...He chose us in Him before the creation of the world to be holy and blameless in His sight."* This verse declares exactly how God sees Christians and declares that it is God's sovereign choice to see Christians that way. Once again, Christians may not understand how God can do that, but the fact is - because the Bible says so - He has chosen to see Christians like that. Importantly, this verse says that God's sovereign choice was made *"...before the creation of the world."* So, His choice clearly cannot be affected by a Christian's day-to-day living – including their day-to-day sins. So, as long as Christians keep their faith (which is given to them by God) in Jesus Christ as both Lord and Saviour, they are *"...in Him"* and, consequently, seen as *"...holy and blameless"* by God – without regard to anything else that is happening in the Christian's life.

Ephesians 5:3 also speaks of *"God's holy people"* and Ephesians 5:25-27 says, *"...Christ loved the church and gave Himself up for her to make her holy, cleansing her by the washing with water through the Word, and to present her to Himself as a radiant church, without stain or wrinkle or any other blemish, but holy and blameless."* A wonderful couple of verses that speak of Christ's great love for His people and tell of what He has achieved for Christians. Colossians 1:22 says the same thing again. *"But now He (God) has reconciled you by Christ's physical body through death to present you holy in His sight, without blemish and free from accusation...."* Once again, Christ's death on the cross is seen as the pivotal event in the process that allows God to view Christians as *"...holy and blameless."*

Colossians 2:13 tells of when Christians were forgiven their sins and contradicts the idea that forgiveness is something for which Christians must ask on a sin-by-sin basis. The verse says, *"When you were dead in your sins and in the uncircumcision of your sinful nature, God made you alive with Christ. He forgave us all our sins."* So, Christians were forgiven of *"...all our sins"* when they were unsaved, when they were still *"dead"* in their sins. In other words, while they were still separated from God – for that is what *"dead"* means. Christians are not forgiven when they become Christians (which is a widespread misunderstanding of Scriptures), they were forgiven when Christ died. The Christian's God-given faith allows them to receive the forgiveness that, since the cross, has been freely available to everyone. It is important to point out that "*all*" sins were forgiven because of the cross – and not just the sins Christians commit before they became Christians.

There are many verses that confirm how God sees the Christian because of Christ's death and resurrection:

<u>Colossians 3:12</u>: *"…as God's chosen people, holy and dearly loved…"*

<u>Titus 3:7</u>: *"…having been justified by His grace, we might become heirs having the hope of eternal life."*

<u>Hebrews 2:11</u>: *"Both the One who makes men holy and those who are made holy are of the same family. So, Jesus is not ashamed to call them brothers."*

<u>Hebrews 10:10</u>: *"And by that (God's) will, we have been made holy through the sacrifice of the body of Jesus Christ once for all."*

<u>Hebrews 13:12</u>: *"And so Jesus also suffered outside the city gate to make the people holy through His own blood."*

<u>1 Peter 2:9</u>: *"But you are a chosen people, a royal priesthood, a holy nation, a people belonging to God,"* NB: This verse uses the present tense saying, "you <u>are</u>" and not "you will be."

<u>1 Peter 3:18</u>: *"For Christ died for sins once for all, the righteous for the unrighteous, to bring you to God."*

Two challenging verses

There are those perhaps who, even after reading these Scriptures, will still look at their own lives and find it just too difficult to accept that the sin issue is completely dealt with as far as God is concerned. But here are two verses that challenge Christians to either accept that God does not see them as sinners, or to accept that they are not saved, not actually Christians! It is as dramatic as that.

1 John 3:6: *"No one who lives in Him keeps on sinning. No one who continues to sin has either seen Him or known Him."* Christians must accept that God sees them as no longer sinning or accept that they have never seen Him or known

Him. As Christians do know the Lord then, from this Scripture, God is saying that they do not, therefore, continue to sin. It should be noted that is it seeing and knowing Jesus that puts Christians in this position, not the Christian's own effort.

1 John 3:8-9: *"He who does what is sinful is of the devil, because the devil has been sinning from the beginning. The reason the Son of God appeared was to destroy the devil's work. No one who is born of God will continue to sin, because God's seed remains in him; he cannot go on sinning, because he has been born of God."* It is as simple as that. A Christian, born of God, "cannot" go on sinning. The Bible does not say "should not" or "will not" it says "cannot."

Christians must accept such Scriptures or challenge the whole trustworthiness of the Bible. There may be Scriptures that Christians find hard to understand – and these verses may fall into that category – but even when they don't understand a Scripture, Christians accept it because it is God's Word.

First conclusion

The question being asked is, "Does a Christian sin." The first conclusion, derived from multiple Scriptures including 1 John 3:9, *"A Christian cannot go on sinning,"* is that from God's perspective, a Christian cannot sin.

PART TWO:
A Christian can do nothing but sin in their own eyes

The reason that some Christians will maintain that they have a responsibility to do something about their sin – confessing, asking for forgiveness, striving not to repeat, and so on – is because they often do not have a proper understanding of their own sinfulness. When Christians gain this understanding, far from bringing condemnation, such knowledge brings liberation from the pressure of sin. It does this because in realising their sinfulness Christians also realise their total dependence upon God's grace. It sets them free from the burden of their sin because, in understanding how great that burden is, Christians realise that Jesus is the only Person able to carry that burden.

A look through various Scriptures illustrates the Christian's sinfulness:

Matthew 5:29-30: *"If your right eye causes you to sin, gouge it out and throw it away. It is better for you to lose one part of your body than for your whole body to be thrown into hell. And if your right hand causes you to sin, cut it off and throw it away. It is better for you to lose one part of your body than for your whole body to go into hell."*

These verses clearly show God's rigid rejection of sin. God does not compromise on sin. Saying "Sorry" just isn't enough. Promising not to commit that sin again makes no difference. The only penalty in the Bible for sin is death – separation from God for eternity. Not only do these verses reveal God's uncompromising attitude to sin, but they also give the first illustration of humanity's ongoing sinfulness. Everyone will have sinned with their eyes and their hands, yet no one has plucked out their eyes or cut off their hands - and none intends to do either of these things. If a Christian wants a relationship with God based on obedience to a set of rules or their own contribution, then they are forced to accept that everyone lives in continuous disobedience.

Matthew 5:48 says, *"Be perfect, therefore, as your heavenly Father is perfect."* This verse is set within the context of a teaching to love everyone equally the same – brothers and sisters in the faith, pagans, *"tax collectors,"* and even enemies. There can be few Christians who can truthfully say that they have loved everyone the same and have never shown any favouritism (1 Timothy 5:21, James 2:1). Each time a Christian fails to love others with the same love they extend to their closest companions, they fall into sin.

Matthew 6:34 also shows how many Christians sin daily and often do not regard it as sin. The verse says, *"Therefore do not worry about tomorrow, for tomorrow will worry about itself."* How many Christians obey this command? How many Christians never worry, but always trust the Lord – for their finances, for their loved ones, for their health, for their emotional needs, their security, and so on? Yet most Christians, when they worry, regard it as "normal" rather than as a sin.

Mark 12:30, *"Love the Lord your God with all your heart and with all your soul and with all your mind and with all your strength."* Never a thought for themselves, never the Christian's own interests. Christians must contrast their own approach and attitude with this command in Mark, and with the Lord's declaration in Luke 22:42, *"...yet not My will, but Yours be done."* Every moment of every day, a Christian's will must be surrendered to God. His purpose, His will, and His Kingdom. Nothing of self. Can any Christian say that this is how they live each day and every day? Every time a Christian places themselves, their loved ones, or personal plans and desires at the center of their thoughts, words, and actions, they sin. Likewise, every moment in which God is not allowed to guide their thoughts, emotions, and behaviors is a moment of sin.

By now Christians ought to be gaining a clearer understanding that they truly are steeped in sin – so steeped that most Christians have no grasp of their sinfulness. So steeped that much of what the Bible calls sin, Christians call "normal."

Mark 12:31 presents another command, and another challenge. It says: "*Love your neighbour as yourself.*" This is one of several similar Scriptures including Philippians 2:3: "*Do nothing out of selfish ambition or vain conceit, but in humility consider others better than yourselves.*" Consider others as better than ourselves! Easy, perhaps, when it is a loved one, or a favourite friend; but what of the neighbour with the annoying habit or the work colleague who obviously doesn't like us? If a Christian loves others as they love themself, they must always treat people as they would treat themself, and as they want others to treat them. Can many Christians claim to always do that? Every time a Christian does not put others before themself, and every time they do not treat others as they would treat themself, they sin.

In Luke 12:33, the Lord commands, "*Sell your possessions and give to the poor.*" Most Christians give from their excess, from what they can afford to give. Most Christians do not give to the point where it affects their lifestyle. This is not a criticism, because most Christians are in the same boat! But it may be something that Christians need to recognise – in terms of gaining an understanding of their sinfulness.

Luke 14:12, "*Then Jesus said to His host, "When you give a luncheon or dinner, do not invite your friends, your brothers or relatives, or your rich neighbours; if you do, they may invite you back and so you will be repaid. But when you give a banquet, invite the poor, the crippled, the lame, the blind, and you will be blessed.""* Based on that, Christians who hold lunch or dinner parties are probably sinning most of the time. How many Christians actively invite the outcast, the socially "odd," the homeless person? How many tend to stick with those with whom they are comfortable? These sorts of commands are all over the New Testament and they simply get ignored by many Christians. An indication of most Christians' sinfulness is that they don't even realise just how much, and how often, they are ignoring the commands of the Lord.

In John 15:12 the Lord says, *"My command is this: Love each other as I have loved you."* Another command to a life of selfless, agape love. Sacrificial, life-surrendering love. Every thought, word and deed that is not inspired by this command is a sin.

Before going on with other Scriptures designed to open the Christians' eyes to their ongoing sinfulness as Christians, it is good to be reminded of the purpose of doing so. The purpose is that in having a better understanding of how sinful Christians are, there will come a total reliance on the grace of the Lord Jesus Christ to make Christians right, and to keep Christians right, with God. Such knowledge will liberate Christians from a life of striving to be a "better" Christian. It will set Christians free from thoughts and feelings of guilt and failure, and it will give Christians a greater confidence before God. So, this is not an exercise in condemnation, but an exercise in liberation from the tyranny of sin and the lies of Satan. Christians are sinners, but they don't need to hide from that fact. Christians simply need to accept God's amazing grace and understand that, through Jesus, the sin issue has been dealt with once and for all.

1 Corinthians 14:26 says, *"What then shall we say, brothers? When you come together, everyone has a hymn, or a word of instruction, a revelation, a tongue or an interpretation. All of these must be done for the strengthening of the church."* Christians should go to church to give to the others who are there. Christians should go to church to give others strength and encouragement through the hymn, word of instruction, revelation, tongue or interpretation that this verse says they have. The reality, however, in most churches, is that everything is done by one or two people from the front, and most of the people sit in the congregation and contribute very little. This is obviously not a Biblical model of Church. Every time Christians are invited to contribute and do not, they deny the truth of this Scripture in 1 Corinthians. So even during what would appear to be an obviously Christian activity – attending church – Christians can be sinning through their silence and non-contribution. As are those who deny the Spirit room to move by not inviting those contributions.

One of the most challenging verses in the Bible, and one that ably illustrates a Christian's sinfulness, is Philippians 2:5 which says: *"Your attitude should be the same as that of Christ Jesus."* It goes on to talk of the humility and sacrificial servanthood that were the hallmarks of the life of Christ. So, a Christian's life should similarly be full of humility towards God and others, and life should be simply an endless succession of acts of sacrificial service. Every time Christians do not manifest that humility (both inwardly as well as outwardly), and every time their lives are not being directed by selfless sacrifice, they sin.

A verse that many Christians may find particularly challenging is Philippians 2:14. It says: *"Do everything without complaining or arguing."* Complaining may prevail in the workplace and, perhaps, arguing within the home; but, either way, there are a lot of Christians who do a fair amount of complaining or arguing – or both! Every time a Christian does either of those things (even if it is only in their thoughts) they sin.

Philippians 4:6, *"Do not be anxious about anything..."* Every time a Christian becomes anxious about anything – finances, health, their children, their job, their home and so on – they sin. Once again, Christians are so sinful by nature that they do not recognise these things as sins but describe them as normal. It is normal to worry, it is normal to be anxious – it is, but only because sin is such a normal part of a Christian's life.

1 Thessalonians 4:7-8 illustrates the depth of a Christian's sin and the depth of God's grace towards that Christian. These verses say: *"For God did not call us to be impure, but to live a holy life. Therefore, he who rejects this instruction does not reject man but God, who gives you His Holy Spirit."* So, to the extent that Christians' lives are not holy, they are rejecting – according to these verses – God Himself. These verses surely illustrate the pointlessness of Christians trying to get rid of sin in their lives through their own efforts. Or of trying to maintain a relationship with God based on saying sorry for sins committed, striving against them, and so on. God demands holiness. The only way Christians can achieve that sinless state is to receive what God, through Jesus, has done for them and accept that the sin issue has been forever dealt with through the cross.

There are many other verses that make the point that the standard God requires is so far above anything a Christian can achieve that believing they contribute anything towards the maintenance of their relationship with God, through the way they live, is foolishness. When Christians understand the extent of their sinfulness, they will understand that they <u>must</u> rely on the grace of God which, as shown earlier, includes the fact that God has chosen to see Christians as sinless. As it says in 1 John 3:9: *"No one who is born of God will continue to sin, because God's seed remains in him; he cannot go on sinning, because he has been born of God."*

So, Christians need to put the sin issue to one side and, in response to God's amazing grace, commit their lives to serving others – rather than wasting any time on supposed shortcomings that they think may stop the Lord from using them.

Final conclusions

1. Christians must know and live in how God sees them to fully benefit from Calvary and to achieve their full potentials in Christ.

2. To help Christians do this - to rely fully upon God's amazing grace – they need to know how utterly sinful they still are.

3. Christians should not necessarily try and understand how God can see them as sinless, when they are so obviously sinful, but they should simply accept, from Romans 4:17, that, *"…God gives life to the dead and calls things that are not as though they were."* God chooses to call Christians holy, righteous, justified, blameless, and so on. Every Christian should live in God's perspective of them.

4. Moses would not accept God's view of his potential and eventually God used Aaron to be His speaker. Gideon accepted God's view of him and freed Israel. Peter (*"Away from me, Lord, for I am a sinful man."*) accepted Christ's view of him and became a *"…fisher of men."*

5. The enemy would have Christians focus on their sins and on their own view of themselves because focusing, instead, on how God sees them will directly impact whether Christians achieve their full potential in Christ.

Question: Does a Christian sin?

Answer: In God's eyes, never; in our eyes, ceaselessly.

The very Good News is that it is God's opinion that counts!

Part Three:

Some commonly mistaught Scriptures

Introduction

Whenever a parable is taught, it is essential to consider the setting in which it is being presented. The question needs to be asked, "Why has Jesus told that story, at that point, to that group of people?" The correct understanding of the parable will lie in the answer to that question. To ignore the setting - that is, what is going on around Jesus at the time of the story - is to risk ending up with a story taken out of context and, possibly, therefore a story incorrectly interpreted and applied.

Whether a parable or a straightforward teaching, when reading the Gospels or the letters of the New Testament, it is also important to understand the culture of first-century Israel, so that misunderstandings do not arise because of incorrect cultural overlays.

For example, many Christians miss the lesson of the transforming power of receiving undeserved love and grace in the parable of the two debtors in Luke 7, particularly as church leaders generally encourage their modern-day listeners to greater personal effort as the way to grow as a Christian. Similarly, many Christians have completely lost the real meaning of the parable of the Good Samaritan in Luke 10, believing it to be a message about good works (lifestyle). Many – probably most -Christians are unaware that Jesus taught a new definition of repentance in His parables in Luke 15, and many Christians are puzzled when the landowner appears to compliment his dishonest manager in Luke 16.

What follows are six very well-known Scriptures which - because of hundreds of years of unquestioning traditional teaching, together with cultural overlays that ignore the Middle Eastern culture within which Jesus was teaching, and because of an overall lack of understanding of the Gospel

– have been mis-taught and misunderstood. The Scriptures following are but a handful of examples from a much wider range of Scriptures that need to be read and understood in the light of both the New Covenant and the culture at the time of their original telling.

As you read the Biblically and culturally correct interpretations of these well-known parables, it will be a helpful exercise to compare them with interpretations you have been taught or heard from others. If the interpretations revealed below are new to you, revisiting your understanding of other Scriptures may prove both enlightening and transformative. As you do, be mindful of teachings that deviate from the Covenant of grace— distorted either by cultural overlays or the uncritical acceptance of long-standing traditional interpretations.

1. The two debtors - Luke 7:40-43

As with all parables, the context within which this parable is told gives the key to the correct understanding of what Jesus is seeking to teach. The parable is set within a longer recounting of events which actually happened. Jesus had been invited to the house of Simon the Pharisee. On entry, Jesus is subjected to a series of calculated insults - these are set out in verses 44-46. The reason for these insults is given when Simon reveals, through his thinking in verse 39, that his motive in inviting Jesus to his house was to make his own assessment as to whether Jesus was a prophet. The woman, in the sequence of events, makes up for Simon's lack of hospitality. It is these contrasting actions that lead to the parable.

In this short parable, Jesus teaches that before God, all are equal. The two debtors in the story are equal because they are both in debt and neither can repay their debt. Both, no matter the size of their individual debt, are dependent upon the mercy of the one to whom they are in debt. The modern application of that lesson is that all Christians are equal in the sight of God. There is great potential for unity when Christians understand that no Christian is better or worse than any other Christian. All Christians are totally, and equally, dependent upon God's mercy.

Although Simon has completely misread the actions of Jesus and the woman, he is able to see, through the parable, that the response to undeserved grace is love from the recipient of grace to the grace-giver. The love towards the grace-giver empowers acts of service, and the greater the grace given, the greater the response from the recipient. This is a simple but powerful message for all Christians. Jesus teaches that as Christians receive grace, far from slipping into slovenly spiritual habits and abuse of grace, the grace received will empower Christians to live out their high calling through acts of service.

These acts of service are a Christian's loving response to God's grace—expressions of gratitude for the grace and forgiveness already received, not efforts to earn more of either.

2. The Good Samaritan - Luke 10:25-37

This is a parable which has been mis-taught for so long that its true meaning has been completely lost to most of the Church. It has generally become a parable that is an encouragement to go out and do good works. The reason for this is, essentially, because the events that led to the telling of the parable have been ignored.

To get a correct interpretation of a parable, it is necessary to look at the circumstances that initiate the telling of the parable. In this case, that means understanding the conversation between Jesus and the lawyer before the telling of the parable.

The first question the lawyer asks Jesus seeks to test Jesus. The Pharisees and the teachers of The Law had a problem with Jesus. He didn't seem to stick to The Law in the way that He, according to their understanding, should do. Jesus healed on the Sabbath, His disciples picked and ate corn on the Sabbath, neither He nor His disciples fasted and neither He nor His disciples observed other aspects of the law. These were all issues upon which the Jewish religious authorities had criticised Jesus. The lawyer approached Jesus to test His stance on the Law—was He upholding it or challenging it?

The lawyer asks the question, *"What must I do to inherit eternal life?"* He asks this because the Rabbis of that time taught that if a person obeyed the Law, then that person would inherit eternal life - in other words, a person could earn their salvation. Jesus knows that the lawyer will, therefore, see obedience to the Law as the way of inheriting eternal life. So, He asks the lawyer what is his understanding of the requirements of the Law, *"What is written in the Law?"* The lawyer's response is to quote Jesus' teaching that the requirement of the Law is to love *"God with all your heart, with all your soul, with all you strength and with all your mind and to love your neighbour as yourself."* Jesus tells the lawyer that he has answered correctly.

Now, though, the lawyer has a problem. He had expected Jesus to give a limited requirement, based on the Law, that he might obey to inherit eternal life. Instead, the answer which the lawyer himself gives is a command that requires unlimited and unreserved love for God and people. The very Law the lawyer turns to for salvation sets a standard that no person can reach.

The lawyer then asks his second question. Having seen, because of his own answer to Jesus' question, a standard in the Law that he cannot reach, he now asks Jesus to narrow down the requirement to a level that the lawyer will be able to meet. *"And who is my neighbour?"* he asks. This is a reasonable question because under Jewish law neither Gentiles nor Samaritans were considered neighbours to the Jews. This lawyer will be expecting to hear something along the lines of, "Your fellow Jew is your neighbour."

It is to answer these questions about the means of justification that Jesus then tells the parable. Understanding this shows that the meaning of the parable cannot be an encouragement to do good works – because good works will never lead to justification before God.

The person who was robbed was left stripped and half dead. What the robbers leave at the roadside is not a Jew, not a Samaritan, not a Gentile, but just a man. He cannot be identified by national or local dress styles because he has been stripped. He cannot speak to identify himself because he is "half-dead." The Jews had different phrases for stages of death and "half-dead" means that the man was unconscious. Anyone coming upon this man would have no way of knowing whether he was Jew or Gentile. Equally, anyone coming upon the man would have no way of knowing how close he was to death.

Under Jewish law, the priest had a legal right to pass this man by. The priest risked becoming "unclean" by contact with the man if he turned out to be a Gentile. The priest also risked becoming "unclean" if he came too close to the man and found him to be dead. So, the listeners of Jesus would not have been at all surprised that the priest *"passed by on the other side."* In fact, they would have been very surprised if the priest had done anything else. In

Western culture, people will expect the priest to help, but that is a cultural overlay.

The Levite, following behind the priest, is not bound by as many ritual restrictions. Yet he hesitates—because by helping the injured man, he risks implying that the priest's interpretation of the Law was flawed. The Levite could reasonably assume that the priest would have helped the man if there had been a legal need to do so. Again, those listening to Jesus would not have been at all surprised by the actions of the Levite who also, *"passed by on the other side."*

This story is being told only a few years after some Samaritans desecrated the Temple in Jerusalem by throwing human bones into it. So, relationships between the two communities were at an all-time low. The listeners to Jesus would have been expecting a Jewish layman to be the hero of His story but, to their surprise, Jesus then introduces a hated Samaritan as the next person in the parable.

The Samaritan is bound by the same Torah (Law) as the priest and the Levite. The attack has taken place between Jerusalem and Jericho, which is in Judea; so, the chances of the wounded man being a fellow Samaritan are just about nil. As the Samaritan is travelling through Judea, on his way to Samaria, it can be easily established that he is probably a trader. He is certainly riding on a donkey and can, therefore, be shown to be relatively well off. He is a prime target for the robbers if they are still in the vicinity. So, the very act of stopping puts the Samaritan at risk.

Jewish Law, giving as it did the right of retaliation, also puts the Samaritan at risk. This is because the Jews, due to the state of Jewish/Samaritan relationships at that time, would have assumed that it was Samaritan robbers who had attacked the wounded Jew. The wounded man's family may well, therefore, have reacted violently against the Samaritan. Despite the very real dangers to himself, the Samaritan feels a deep compassion for the wounded man - a compassion which is immediately translated into action. It is here that one can begin to detect the role of God in humanity's salvation.

The Samaritan is in no way responsible for what has happened to the wounded man, yet he compensates for all that has happened to him. The Samaritan compensates for the lack of compassion of both the priest and the

Levite and he compensates for the robbers - they robbed the man, and the Samaritan pays for him (at the inn). All the others, in one way or another, abandon the man; the Samaritan takes him to the inn and sees that he is taken care of. It costs the Samaritan time, money, effort and risk of personal danger.

The Samaritan is a totally unknown stranger, yet despite the costs and the dangers he freely demonstrates unexpected, unconditional and unlimited love to the one in need. In this story, Jesus is identifying Himself through the actions of the Samaritan. They both, the one in the parable and the One in reality, are an unexpected source of salvation, come to heal, save and restore, accepting possible misunderstanding and hostility, and paying the price themselves for the salvation and restoration of the needy.

In summary: The parable is NOT an encouragement to do good works for one's neighbour. The parable is told within the context of a conversation about self-justification. Jesus answers the lawyer's questions about self-justification by showing the standard God requires from those who seek to be right with Him by their own efforts. The problem for the lawyer, and all people, is that God's standard is beyond reach. Jesus is pointing out, not the need for good works, but the need every human being has of a Saviour.

The parables of Luke 15
The background to all three parables in Luke 15 is that Jesus was being accused, and reviled, by the Pharisees and the teachers of the Law. The reason for their accusations and revulsion was that Jesus was welcoming "*sinners*" and was even eating with them. In the Middle East in the time of Jesus, to eat with someone was to honour that person. To invite someone to share a meal was to offer peace, trust and brotherhood. Jesus is really identifying with the "*sinners*" and, in effect, saying, "I totally accept you as a brother. I am willing to sit down and have table fellowship with you."

This is a radical thing that Jesus is doing. These are not "repentant sinners," as the Pharisees understand that phrase, with whom Jesus is dining. They are still tax collectors, possibly prostitutes, and other recognised "*sinners*." Jesus, in dining with tax collectors and "*sinners*," is making a powerful statement about God's attitude towards those whom the self-righteous reject. It was to illustrate God's attitude to sinners and to challenge the rejection by the self-righteous of those who were still seen as sinners that Jesus then told three parables. The first two demonstrate God's attitude toward sinners and the third presents the sinner with a choice of whether to respond to God's gracious offer.

3. The lost sheep - Luke 15:1-7

Jesus opens the parable with *"Suppose one of you has a hundred sheep and loses one of them."* King David and many other Old Testament figures had been shepherds, and many prophecies speak of God acting as a shepherd for His people. Despite the honoured position of shepherds in Jewish history and Scripture, the Pharisees of Jesus' time had declared shepherds unclean. For this reason, they would have been offended by Jesus' opening statement which likened them to shepherds. It was a direct challenge to their attitude to others.

Jesus went on, *"Does he not leave the ninety-nine in the open country and go after the lost sheep until he finds it."* Jesus is beginning to explain God's attitude towards sinners. Jesus is revealing, to those who asked the question, *"Why is He eating with sinners?"* just how much God cares for every individual, and the lengths to which God will go to find that lost sinner. Jesus uses the example of a lost sheep for different reasons. One of the reasons is that a sheep when lost will sit down and not move. It will not attempt to find its way home. It is, and must be, therefore, the shepherd's responsibility to find the sheep. The shepherd must keep searching until he finds the sheep or the sheep will die. The shepherd is, in fact, the lost sheep's only hope of life.

These are simple but powerful illustrations of the truths of the Gospel. God came looking for lost sinners. God will keep searching out lost sinners. He must, because, He is the only hope that lost sinners have. Sinners cannot contribute anything towards altering their state of lostness. The Gospel of Grace is being clearly laid out.

When the sheep is found, the shepherd *"...joyfully puts it on his shoulders and goes home."* The searching for and finding of lost sinners is God's responsibility. A lost sinner can do nothing about their lostness. When a *"sinner"* becomes a Christian there is a tendency to take on the burden of ensuring their ongoing salvation: A striving to keep on the *"...narrow road that leads to life"* (Matt 7:14). That striving, that fear of going astray, is the cause of endless unhappiness and division within the Church. Yet, in the parable of the lost sheep, Jesus is clearly teaching that it is the shepherd's responsibility to get the sheep safely back home - which, for the Christian, is Christ ensuring the Christian's eternal security for the rest of their life on earth. Not only is it the shepherd's responsibility but, Jesus teaches that the carrying of that burden is something He undertakes, *"joyfully."*

The shepherd has made no demands of the sheep; but has accepted fully the consequences of the sheep becoming lost and, additionally, the responsibility for the restoration of the sheep into its community. That is God's wonderful message of salvation to humanity. God, making no demands of lost sinners, accepts fully the consequences of a person's lostness (the cross) and accepts fully the responsibility of restoring a person into communion with Himself (the giving of the Holy Spirit, guaranteeing the Christian's inheritance).

When a lost sinner is brought into the community of Believers, that person is not there by their own efforts but by God's, and the welcome and acceptance that new Christians receive should reflect that truth.

When the shepherd had restored the lost sheep to the village community, he called all his friends and neighbours to celebrate the finding and restoration of that lost sheep. When a lost sinner is saved, let the community of Christians celebrate - rather than looking at any apparent shortcomings that may still be in the new Christian. Let the community of Christians allow Christ to carry the burden of the new convert, rather than sowing fears of a lost salvation over some sinful habit that may not yet have been overcome or set aside.

Jesus finishes the parable by saying, *"I tell you that in the same way there will be more rejoicing in heaven over one sinner who repents than over ninety-nine righteous persons who do not need to repent."* Here, Jesus is obviously likening the one lost sheep to one repentant sinner. He is beginning to reveal a new understanding of what it is to be repentant.

To understand this new revelation of repentance, the question needs to be asked, "What did the lost sheep do that allows Jesus to liken it to a repentant sinner?" An examination of the parable shows that the sheep, essentially, did two things. Firstly, the sheep got lost. Every Christian accepts that they, prior to salvation, were lost. Secondly, the sheep accepted being found. The sheep allowed the shepherd to take responsibility for restoring the sheep to its community. Through these two actions, the sheep effectively acknowledge the shepherd as both Savior and Lord.

For the Rabbis, repentance was a condition to be met before grace could be offered. Jesus teaches that this is not the case. The sheep, and equally the sinner, does nothing to prompt the shepherd's diligent searching and restoration except to become lost and, subsequently, accept being found. This, then, is the new definition of repentance - the acceptance of God's work on humanity's behalf.

This is entirely in keeping with the Gospel of Jesus Christ, within which the responsibility for a sinner's salvation and safekeeping rests completely with God.

4. The lost coin - Luke 15:8-10

Again, Jesus starts by attacking the prejudice of the day by making, in a male-dominated society, a woman the central figure in the story. Jesus will not accept attitudes that regard any part of society as anything less than equal to all other parts of society.

A peasant village, at the time of Jesus, would be self-supporting in terms of crops, animals, skills and a system of bartering. Cash would have been quite rare, so the loss of a coin would be a serious event. Jesus is using illustrations which show the importance and value that God attaches to a lost sinner. The coin, in the village community, has a much greater value than just its face value. God sees within each person a far greater value than that which is apparent from just the outside.

This parable contains the same main points as the lost sheep. There is the grace of the thorough search, carried on relentlessly until the lost one is found. There is the joy of finding and restoring the lost coin. The cost of the search, carried out by the woman, is illustrated. Finally, Jesus likens the lost coin to a repentant sinner and, in so doing, illustrates His new definition of repentance - the acceptance of lostness and the acceptance of being found.

5. The lost Son - Luke 15:11-24

A lack of understanding of Middle Eastern culture during Jesus' time often leads to misinterpretations of the true message He was teaching. This parable, for example, has become known as the Parable of the Prodigal, or Lost, Son. In fact, there are two lost sons at the beginning of this parable; lost in the sense that both are out of relationship with their father.

Christians are generally taught to identify with the younger son. They have lived life under their own power and direction, realised it was leading them nowhere, and returned to their father. Those listening to Jesus would have heard the parable completely differently. They would have been encouraged to identify with the older son. The younger son is a complete story and, as such, requires no response from the listeners. The older son, on the other hand, is still out of relationship with his father when the story ends. The listener is supposed to identify with that older son and decide their own reaction. Will they accept the father's invitation back into the family - not as a servant, but as a son?

This, then, is a parable for the unbeliever, not for the Christian. It does, for the Christian, illustrate major points in Jesus' teaching and, from that point of view, it is very important; but it requires no response from a Christian. A modern understanding that the older son represents a jealous, or otherwise upset, Christian can be quickly shown to be wrong by the fact that, at the end of the story, there is no father/son relationship between the father and the older son - clearly, the older son is unsaved at this point.

The parable opens with the younger son requesting, *"Father, give me my share of the estate."* That which was due to the younger son would not come to him until his father had died. In making this request, the younger son is in effect saying, "Look, I can't wait for you to die; I want what's mine now." It is a stark illustration of the total breakdown in the relationship between the father and the son.

In Jewish culture when Jesus was here, the family was the most important unit within society. The listeners would have expected the older brother to have protested loudly at such a heartless request. Not only should he have strongly rebuked his younger brother, but he should also have declared that he certainly wouldn't be taking his share of the inheritance until the due time. Instead, the older brother remains perfectly silent. That silence would have had a profound meaning to Jesus' listeners showing, as it did, the equally non-existent relationship between the father and the older son.

The older son, by his silence, accepts the division of the estate and so receives his half; thus, confirming that he too cannot wait for the father to die. The only difference between the two brothers at this point is that the younger brother has voiced his feelings, whereas the older brother has yet to do so. Within the father's response, is an amazing illustration of God's love. The father had the legal right to reprimand his younger son - even to the point of having him stoned for rebellion, as laid down in the Law of Moses. Instead, the father's love is sufficient even to allow for the son's rejection of his father.

After the younger son has spent all his money on wild living in a Gentile country, he encounters hard times. There is a famine. Listeners to Jesus would have been familiar with famines and the disastrous impact they had. They would also have been aware of the acutely vulnerable position in which this young Jew found himself: Without money, without friends, a Jew in a Gentile land and the grip of a famine. Despite his dire circumstances, his pride is still not broken. He thinks he can sort out his problems and obtains a job - albeit, feeding pigs, which were unclean animals to Jews. Eventually, the son realises that despite trying to sort out his problems, he is still slowly starving to death.

In verse 18 of the passage, he comes up with a plan. He plans, as revealed in verse 19, to go back to his father and say, *"I am no longer worthy to be called your son, make me like one of your hired men."* Today, this is often taught as repentance—a turning around, a return to the father. It needs to be stated most clearly that, according to the teachings of Jesus, the younger son is entirely unrepentant at this stage. The younger son thinks that the money he has squandered, and the way he has lived, is the problem between him and his father. He has not yet realised that it is the broken relationship which is the real issue. Seeing the money as the issue, the younger son plans is to work for his father and, out of his wages, pay him back. Thus, the younger son is to be the author of his own salvation. That is not repentance!

Additionally, as one of his father's hired men, he won't be living in the family home because, hired men do not do that. So, under the younger son's plan, the split between father and son will remain. The only purpose of paying the money back is so that the younger son can return to his home village without fear of punishment either from his father or from the other villagers who, by this time, will obviously have heard about what has happened. The young man has no idea that he needs to receive grace.

On seeing the returning son, the father is filled with compassion. He runs through the village streets to meet his son. In that culture and in those times, no man would run in public; it would be considered undignified, even humiliating. The more stately a man walked, the more he gained respect. The father, though, knows that the village is angry with his son. By squandering his inheritance in a Gentile land and by working as a pig-herder, the young man has disgraced his whole village. The father must reach the son before any of the villagers do.

This is a powerful illustration of God's love for humanity and of the cross in particular. The father accepts the public humiliation brought on by running to save his son - just as Jesus later accepted the public humiliation of the cross to offer salvation to humanity. The father in this story, and Christ on the cross, made the reconciliation totally public. For all to see, the father hugs the son and kisses him. Nothing is held back by the father; he wants everyone to know that he is offering the son, without any conditions, any reprimand, any questions, full restoration into the family in the position of a son.

The son came back with the intention of being the author of his own salvation. He came back thinking that his lifestyle and the money were the issue. He came back with the attitude of a servant, "I will work for you." He meets with this overwhelming demonstration of love and acceptance from the father and realises that the issue the father wants to be sorted out is the broken relationship - and that only the father has the right to offer restoration of that relationship.

Now the son begins to realise his need to receive grace, for here is a situation which is beyond his ability to change. The son knows what it has cost the father to run through the village. He knows what it has cost the father to publicly hug and kiss him. The son then faces a decision. Does he continue with his plan to work for his father and, through his own efforts, pay back his father; or does he accept this freely offered, unconditional restoration into sonship? Is he going to repent, as Jesus teaches it, and accept being found? In verse 21 there is repentance. The son declares his unworthiness of being called a son - something all Christians can identify with - but drops his planned offer to work for his father. He accepts the position of a son which, being undeserved, is offered through grace.

Jesus is teaching here that what bothers God is the broken relationship between Him and His children. The way people live is not an issue - because Jesus has borne the penalty for all sins. In the story, receiving the father's love turned a would-be servant into a son. If Christians wish to know whether they have truly grasped grace, they need to only ask themselves the question, "Am I living as a servant, or as a son? Am I seeking to, in some way, 'work' for God - or am I receiving the freely offered position of a son?" If there are lingering doubts within the mind of a Christian that somehow, they must "do something" for God then that Christian needs to delve deeper into the wonders of grace. God makes no demands of any person except faith (which He gives us) in terms of a person's restoration into a relationship with Him.

At the end of the parable Jesus again illustrates the joy that there is in heaven when a lost sinner repents. The father kills the fatted calf and invites the whole village to join him in this celebration of a son who *"...was dead and is alive again, he was lost and is found."* This joy of restoration could not have occurred unless the son had accepted grace.

A New Covenant Christian must live under New Covenant **repentance**, as taught by Jesus, and not Old Covenant repentance which was taught by the Rabbis and which placed a heavy burden on people. Salvation is a gift, freely offered through **grace**. It is a gift which only God can offer. A person must accept their lostness, realising that there is nothing they can do about it, and accept being found. God's love is freely offered and is a love that seeks and suffers in order to save. God and the angels of heaven share the **joy** of finding and restoring a lost sinner. A relationship with His children is God's desire. God offers **sonship**, not servanthood. The older son, still living as a servant, has yet to decide his response.

6. The Shrewd Manager - Luke 16:1-8

This parable is told by Jesus to the disciples; thus, it is a parable for the saved, not for the unsaved. It is a parable which deals with the issues of both salvation and ongoing sanctification and, as such, cannot be applied to the unsaved. In the parable, the master is a wealthy landowner with a manager who has the authority to carry out the business of the estate. The debtors are almost certainly men who have rented the estate land and who have agreed to pay a fixed amount of produce for the yearly rent. The villagers have shown they respect the landowner by the fact that someone has alerted him about his dishonest manager.

When the master says to the manager, *"What is this I hear about you?"* the manager makes no reply. Those listening to Jesus would have expected this silence. The manager doesn't know how much the master knows; his best bet, at this stage, is to keep quiet and hope the master doesn't know too much. The master, though, then goes on and fires the manager. The manager remains quiet. The audience would have expected the manager, now with nothing to lose, to loudly protest his innocence. In keeping quiet the manager is effectively acknowledging his guilt.

The manager is also acknowledging other things through his silence; he is acknowledging that the master knows what has been going on, that he is a master who demands obedience and that he is a master who punishes disobedience. The manager has realised that there is no point in offering excuses to such a master. The manager, though, has also seen another very important aspect in his master's character. Although the manager has been stealing from the master, he is not sent to jail - which the social and judicial norms of that time would have demanded. The manager has seen in this encounter two very important aspects of the master's character: firstly, he is a master who exacts justice, and secondly, he is a master who tempers justice with mercy.

The manager now has a problem. He has lost his job and he does not know how he will survive. He eliminates various options and then comes up with a solution. He plans to reduce the size of the debts due to the master from those who are renting his land. As the manager, it is his job to negotiate these rents, so that he will get credit from the debtors for obtaining the reductions - and that will ensure his well-being now that his job has ended. He must act quickly before the debtors find out that he no longer has authority to reduce their rents. The manager carries out his plan and then delivers the newly altered books to his master.

The master now has two choices. His first option is to go into the village and tell them it was all a mistake and the reductions were not valid. If he does this the debtors could become angry with him for his apparent meanness. His second option is to keep silent, absorb the losses, and receive the praise being given to him for his generosity. That praise is not misplaced, because the listener has already heard that the master is generous and merciful—demonstrated in how he treated his manager.

The master's reaction is to compliment the manager on his shrewdness. In the RSV, the master says, *"You are a wise fellow."* One of the Old Testament definitions of wisdom is "the instinct for self-preservation." In the Old Testament, *"wisdom"* is also used to mean "cleverness." It is in this context that the master compliments the manager. The master is, in effect, saying, "Well done. You are clever enough to see where your only hope of self-preservation lay, and you have taken it." The master is complimenting the manager, not for his dishonesty, but for his instinct for survival which lay behind his plan.

The master, thus, becomes the instrument of the manager's initial salvation - in that he did not send the manager to jail - and he then becomes the instrument of the manager's ongoing salvation, or sanctification, by absorbing the cost of the manager's repeated dishonesty.

The disciples - and Christians today - are being encouraged by Jesus to have the same daring hope in God's mercy and generosity - daring to believe that the same grace which initially saves will, also, eternally ensure the Believer's well-being. And it will.

The manager was a sinner - as is every human being. The manager had received his master's mercy - as has the Christian. The manager had no means of providing for his own future well-being; just as, despite being saved, the Christian cannot then keep right with God through their own efforts. The manager entrusted his future well-being to his master's ongoing mercy; the Christian is being taught by Jesus to do likewise. The master commended the manager for seeing where his only hope of well-being lay and for his shrewdness in then resting all his hope on the ongoing mercy of the master. Jesus is teaching that the Christian is, far from taking advantage of God's mercy, being equally shrewd in resting all their hope on God's ongoing mercy.

Conclusion

It is not only in the parables that we can see examples of mis-taught Scriptures.

When a Christian repents as Jesus defines repentance, understands grace as Jesus taught and demonstrated grace and identifies all the gifts – Jesus, eternal life, the Holy Spirit, forgiveness, sanctification and so much more that God has given us – they will be so much better able to interpret the Scriptures correctly, live out their high calling and enjoy a closer relationship with the Lord.

Part Four:

Unbiblical practices in Church

Introduction

Earlier chapters have illustrated how Christianity, overall, has moved away from Biblical doctrines and what now passes as Christianity is based more on traditional understandings, which are often corrupted by cultural overlays, and wrong teaching, spread in some cases, over hundreds of years.

These incorrect understandings and teachings have led to or contributed to, erroneous practices within church services. This chapter will highlight some of those erroneous practices.

The purpose of highlighting these erroneous modern practices in the Church is not to criticize or be mean-spirited, but to reveal a sobering truth: the Church is failing in what is perhaps its most vital calling, which is to bring both Christians and non-believers into the presence of God, and to provide God with an environment within which He can genuinely move upon His people, drawing them closer, revealing more of Himself and inspiring and empowering His Church - from the individual to the whole Church - to go out and reveal God in the world outside of the church building and meetings.

In each case, I will look at a modern practice – each one having been experienced countless times within many churches across several countries over the approximately 40 years I have been a Christian - and I will present Scriptures and examples from the Bible that illustrate how that common practice is not in accord with Biblical teaching.

The examination of modern church practices presented here is not an exhaustive list. For the sake of brevity, it does not address the issue of denominationalism or the false doctrines, teachings, and practices associated with specific denominations.

The hierarchical priesthood

The first, and visually most obvious, issue to examine is that of the established hierarchical priesthood in place in both major denominations – the Anglican (Protestant) and the Catholic denominations, with similar regimes in many smaller denominations. This priesthood is a glaring example of the absorption of Old Covenant doctrine into the New Covenant – a matter addressed earlier in this book.

When God instituted the Old Covenant, the Law of Moses, it included the establishment of the priesthood. Aaron, the brother of Moses, was appointed High Priest and there were others who acted as priests and Temple servants in various ways. Many rituals were created to ensure the holiness of the priests and of the Temple in which they served. The priests were an elevated group of people, above the ordinary Israelites. They had magnificent robes and could undertake duties in which no ordinary Israelite could participate.

But when Jesus came, He warned His followers, Luke 20:46, *"Beware of the teachers of the law. They like to walk around in flowing robes and love to be greeted with respect in the marketplaces and have the most important seats in the synagogues and the places of honour at banquets."* The priesthood had become corrupted and lost sight of its purpose and role.

The very thing that Jesus warned against is now an embedded part of the Church. Modern Christianity has a class set apart, the priesthood, to lead "ordinary" Christians – in the same way that the Jews had a class set aside to lead Temple worship and carry out various duties and rituals from which ordinary Jews were excluded. Under the Old Covenant, this was acceptable because it was what God had established when He gave the Law to Moses and Israel; however, under the New Covenant, such an arrangement is no longer acceptable because it has no Biblical mandate. Yet we have a class of Christians who are elevated above "ordinary" Christians.

Church leaders today are generally given a title – from the seemingly humble Pastor to the grand Archbishop or Pope. A multitude of available titles include, Minister, Vicar, Father, Archdeacon, Bishop, Reverend, Cardinal and so on. Even the widespread use of the title Reverend – coming as it does from the Latin word "reverendus" (meaning: "one who must be respected") - is entirely inappropriate for a servant of Christ and a leader within any Christian church.

The special robes that many leaders wear, particularly in the larger denominations, are clearly contrary to the Lord's teaching in Matthew 12:38, *"As He taught, Jesus said, 'Watch out for the teachers of the law. They like to walk around in flowing robes and be greeted with respect in the marketplaces…."* Jesus issued a warning to His early followers to beware of such people.

The titles, the robes, the demand for respect (one who must be respected), and the special seats (not in synagogues but churches) suggest (a) a lack of understanding of and/or obedience to Biblical instructions, (b) a lack of understanding of the character and life of Jesus Christ and (c) a resultant loss of awareness for an attitude of humility and servanthood at all times.

Those leaders who engage with special titles, special garments and a willingness to be elevated above others, have lost contact with their moorings of Biblical teachings on the characteristics and personality traits required of leaders, and the clear, unequivocal Biblical teachings on how to conduct oneself if in a position of leadership within Christ's Church.

One of the greatest aspects of grace is that it is the Great Leveller. No-one is better than anyone else, no one is worse than anyone else. There is no call or basis for a class to be elevated and set above other Christians. Romans 2:11 declares, *"God does not show favouritism."* God has not established an elite group to minister before Him and lead His Church. Revelation 1:5-6 makes it even clearer, *"To Him who loves us and has freed us from our sins by His blood, and has made us to be a kingdom and priests to serve His God and Father…"* Christians are all priests in the Kingdom of God.

The hierarchical priesthood places limits upon what "ordinary" Christians may do in the Church. So, for example, they may not administer the breaking of bread (communion), they may not baptise others, they may not offer absolution for sins – and so on. Absolutely NONE of this has any basis in the Scriptures and, in fact, opposes what the Bible teaches and demonstrates. The current cohort of priests is not to be blamed for this. It is a system that has been in place and developing for somewhere in the region of 1,700 years. But it is time to make our churches Biblical if we wish to operate in accordance with God's will for His Church.

All Church leaders – clergy and otherwise

The New Testament gives very clear instructions about who may be a leader in a church.

1 Timothy 3:1-13: *"Here is a trustworthy saying: Whoever aspires to be an overseer desires a noble task. Now the overseer is to be above reproach, faithful to his wife, temperate, self-controlled, respectable, hospitable, able to teach, not given to drunkenness, not violent but gentle, not quarrelsome, not a lover of money. He must manage his own family well and see that his children obey him, and he must do so in a manner worthy of full respect. (If anyone does not know how to manage his own family, how can he take care of God's church?) He must not be a recent convert, or he may become conceited and fall under the same judgment as the devil. He must also have a good reputation with outsiders, so that he will not fall into disgrace and into the devil's trap. In the same way, deacons are to be worthy of respect, sincere, not indulging in much wine, and not pursuing dishonest gain. They must keep hold of the deep truths of the faith with a clear conscience. They must first be tested; and then if there is nothing against them, let them serve as deacons."*

Similarly,

Titus 1:6-9: *"An elder must be blameless, faithful to his wife, a man whose children believe and are not open to the charge of being wild and disobedient. Since an overseer manages God's household, he must be blameless—not overbearing, not quick-tempered, not given to drunkenness, not violent, not pursuing dishonest gain. Rather, he must be hospitable, one who loves what is good, who is self-controlled, upright, holy and disciplined. He must hold firmly to the trustworthy message as it has been taught, so that he can encourage others by sound doctrine and refute those who oppose it."*

There are other, shorter, instructions for leaders and elders – including within the teachings of Jesus, Himself. When the Church accepts anyone as a leader who does not meet the standards laid out in the two Scriptures above, they are outside of the will of God for the church and open it up to all sorts of spiritual and other problems. Obeying these commands on leadership will potentially create problems for the Church. For example, when the Scriptures talk about being the husband of but one wife, it is talking about one man and one woman – so that rules out anyone who has been divorced and re-married, and it rules out those in a same-sex relationship. Some churches may view this as a difficult decision, but it is a simple choice of honouring God's Word or not honouring God's Word. We cannot expect God's blessing, as a Church, when we blatantly disregard, and thus dishonour, God's Word. Maybe being faced with such a choice will cause the Church, and churches individually, to choose the direction in which the leaders and congregation wish to take that church.

However, the commands and criteria are not all about the marital state of the leader. The parenting skills of the leader must also be under scrutiny. Are the leader's children obedient, are they respectful, do they hold to the truths of the faith? It has long been the norm that children go to church when they are young but start to drift away as they get to around mid-teens. This can also be true of the children of leaders, at which point the leader should, to honour God's Word, step down.

Issues like this create some difficulties for all concerned – but the church must face this uncomfortable choice: Honour God's Word and face conflict, or disregard and dishonour God's Word and avoid conflict. For too long, many – perhaps most – churches have chosen the latter path. This alone will explain much about why the Church is now seen as powerless and irrelevant.

Much of the Church's leadership – in all denominations – is indeed separated from their moorings and adrift in a sea of misunderstanding, and lack of knowledge and disobedience. And, as the Bible makes it clear: where the shepherd leads, the flock will follow.

Jesus demonstrated complete humility, and complete respect and obedience towards His Father. So should all who dare to – or aspire to – set themselves up as leaders within the Church. The Church must regain the courage and integrity to submit all aspiring leaders to the selection criteria outlined in the passages above from Titus, 1 Timothy, and Matthew – as well as the other teachings on leadership within the Bible.

Where this criteria is ignored, a situation can arise, as happened in September 2024, where the global leader of the Roman Catholic Church, the Pope, can inform a public audience that, "All religions are paths to God"; and where a third of Anglican clergy in the United Kingdom do not believe in the physical resurrection of Jesus, only half believe in the virgin birth of Jesus, and only half believe Jesus is the only way of salvation.

Where the shepherds lead, the flock will follow.

The structure of church services

The very structure of a modern church service dictates that error now dominates within most churches in that services are controlled by the clock and, therefore, not by the Spirit. It is almost as though churches have forgotten that they exist to wait on God, glorify God, meet with God, be blessed and empowered by God, as well as be a blessing and encouragement to each other.

It is indeed Biblical to have order within a church service, but that order should never extend to limiting the time that God is given to move amongst His people. A church service today is sufficiently predictable that it is hard to imagine any Christian arriving for a service with a sense of wonder at what the Lord may do or say within the service. Church services have become routine: arrival, greetings, a short opening prayer with the usual requests for God to bless the Christians' time together etc, worship (up to around a 40-minute block or, for more traditional churches, split across several individual hymns), announcements, sermon, prayers, closing song/hymn. Some variations apply with, for example, the exact order of the activities, with communion/breaking bread and possibly a collection being included, but essentially everyone knows what to expect, what order to expect it in, how long each segment will last and what time they can expect to go home for Sunday lunch.

Yet the Bible commands that, having arrived at the house of God, Christians should, Psalm 27:14, *"Wait for the Lord; be strong and take heart and wait for the Lord"* and in Psalm 46:10 God commands, *"Be still, and know that I am God…"* We need to regain a humility before God that recognises our place before God and submits to waiting upon Him.

Today, there seems to be neither room, nor time, nor even expectation for the Holy Spirit to take over—so He doesn't

The arrival period

The erroneous practices start before the service even commences. The pre-service time, when the congregants/members start to gather, seems often to be a time of social chit-chat, banter, highly active children, cups of coffee, and wanderings around the church as those present greet one another. This is generally done in the name of building and strengthening the sense of community experienced by the regular attendees – a sense of being "a family church." A commendable goal, perhaps, but not a Biblical method for achieving that goal.

The problem that has developed through this approach is that there is no sense of reverence, no sense of awe, as Christians enter the house of God. The Lord promised that *"Where two or three gather together in My Name, there I am with them."* (Matthew 18:20). The type of social interactions and physical activity before a service does not demonstrate any sense of awareness or belief that God is present within the church. No doubt, those present are not chatting and interacting in such a manner through any sense of unbelief – just that the modern Church has lost what it is to experience the presence of God.

So those gathering for a church service do not expect to use the pre-service time for prayerful preparation for the service, for conversations with God rather than with the person sitting beside them. Quiet contemplation is missed as others come to engage in conversation the one sitting quietly alone seeking the presence of God – and that interruption is done with the best of motives, to be welcoming and friendly. Important though that is, it is not as important as allowing all present to seek God's presence.

Ecclesiastes 5:1-2 contains these instructions, *"Guard your steps when you go to the house of God. Go near to listen rather than to offer the sacrifice of fools, who do not know that they do wrong. Do not be quick with your mouth, do not be hasty in your heart to utter anything before God. God is in heaven and you are on earth, so let your words be few."*

This reinforces the idea of a required reverence in the house of the Lord – the church. When we are reminded of whose presence we have come into, it is astonishing that we may consider social chit-chat to be acceptable. Our words should be few out of reverence towards God.

David had the right approach when he wrote, in Psalm 19, *"Let the words of my mouth and the meditation of my heart Be acceptable in Your sight, O Lord, my strength and my Redeemer."* This may be a suitable reflection and prayer, offered up upon entering the church, to focus minds and hearts on the things of heaven and not the worldly topics that generally make up the pre-service words of church attendees.

A point to consider, in addition to the Scriptures above, is this: a church should be made up of a cross-section of society. So, there may be some wealthy people, some struggling, some genuinely poor; there may be some employed, some unemployed, some retired, some unable to work for whatever reason; there may be young, middle-aged, elderly; there may be some from other cultures; some "just seeking" and some who have been Christians for 30 or 40 years or even longer.

Either we gather into cliques of those we know and with whom we are comfortable, or we reach out in Christian fellowship to all and sundry. But how can we engage in meaningful conversation with anyone and everyone in such a diverse melting pot of people? The answer is simple: we all have one thing in common with everyone else in the church – faith in (or an openness to faith in) Jesus Christ. If our conversations are spiritual – about the Lord, about a Bible passage we found useful during the week, about a prayer needed or a prayer answered and so on – then such conversations will be edifying, can involve any and all, and meet the Biblical requirement of being acceptable in God's sight (Psalm 19 above).

As Paul put it in Romans 1:11-12, *"For I long to see you, that I may impart to you some spiritual gift, so that you may be established - that is, that I may be encouraged together with you by the mutual faith both of you and me."*

I was once part of a fellowship in London that had everyone from a chief scientist of a large industrial company to homeless people still battling drugs and other such issues among those who regularly gathered together. Most of us had nothing in common with each other except our faith so we decided, as a fellowship, that we would only talk about spiritual matters whilst we were together. It put Jesus at the heart of our time together, and it enabled people, whatever their station in this world, to talk equally and confidently with each other. It was edifying and uplifting. Sometimes, words were few, so people would pray together, or open the Scriptures and read a passage together – united by that one unifying factor, our individual and communal faith in Christ. And the Lord greatly blessed those fellowship meetings.

This approach, far from being restrictive, accords with the Biblical view in 1 Corinthians 14:26, of what should happen within a Christian gathering, *"When you come together, each of you has a hymn, or a word of instruction, a revelation, a tongue or an interpretation. Everything must be done so that the church may be built up."*

Out with idle chit-chat, replace it with spiritual input and sharing, and the Church will be built up.

Worship

It seems that, for many today, no church can be considered worth attending unless it has a worship band/group. Guitars and drums are an absolute necessity, as is a lead singer and a good sound system.

A problem in worship arises because of the now well-developed distance between Biblical Christianity and what happens and is taught in churches so that most Christians cannot differentiate between worldly emotions and spirituality. This means that when the worship group pumps out 40 minutes of popular songs, stoking the emotions of the congregants through floor-stomping, hand-clapping rhythms and vocals, endlessly repeated, alternated with heart-tugging lyrics of the deepest love that the church attendees have for God, those present are emotionally high by the end. The spiritual immaturity of the congregation – witnessed to by these events, including the dutiful obedience to the endless repetitions that are demanded by the band, and the likely unquestioning acceptance of the trite and often unbiblical lyrics of many of the songs – means those present will assume, incorrectly, their emotional reaction is the Holy Spirit moving within them individually and the church as a whole.

Anyone who has ever attended a music concert will recognise the emotional response generated by the numbers present, the atmosphere of the event and the impact of the music. Years ago, I attended the Last Night of the Proms in the Royal Albert Hall in London. What I am writing about in churches today is exactly what I, and everyone present at The Last Night, experienced.

By the end of the popular section of patriotic songs such as "Rule Britannia" and "Land of Hope and Glory," performed every year at the end of the Last Night's concert, everyone present had a very strong feelgood reaction to the music and songs – all based on the foot-stomping, handclapping music and heart-tugging lyrics of the songs, aided by the multiple repetitions of the more well-known choruses.

But I don't think anyone's bosom was swelling with a wave of heart-felt patriotism or a yearning for the re-establishment of Empire – we all just felt happy and emotionally high, both being induced by the atmosphere, the crowd present providing a sense of community and belonging, and the orchestra's expert use of their music to beneficially manipulate the emotions and reactions of those present.

What goes on in so many churches today is no different.

No one is filled with a sufficient fervour for God, or the Gospel, that they experience a change of direction in their life from that moment forward, they simply feel emotionally high. Not necessarily wrong, but certainly not Holy Spirit created.

The other serious error within the worship of many churches today is the willingness - through lack of Biblical knowledge and lack of individual Christians thinking things through for themselves - to sing songs that are simply unbiblical. When leading a fellowship in London, and the same process occurred when I moved to Devon and led a fellowship there, a group of those attending went through the most popular book of hymns and Christian songs used by churches at that time. The book had several hundred songs within it but, through careful examination and by comparison with the Bible, the overwhelming majority of songs were rejected as unsuitable. Sometimes it was because the lyrics could be clearly identified as contrary to Biblical teaching, sometimes because they were "Me" focused and not God-focused, and sometimes because they were just a spiritually meaningless collection of words similar to the love songs that groups/bands use to sell their music to love-sick teenagers!

In the process of producing a mass of these popular songs, many churches have abandoned almost completely the great hymns of earlier times - an absolute host of hymns that, literally, sing out the Gospel story.

The Church is weaker, and increasingly open to error, for these three reasons within what passes today for worship.

The Church has lost sight of the meaning of worship but, providentially, the Bible gives a very simple and very clear definition for those who truly seek to worship the Lord. Romans 12:1, *"Therefore, I urge you, brothers and sisters, in view of God's mercy, to offer your bodies as a living sacrifice, holy and pleasing to God - this is your true and proper worship."*

These words from Paul really need little to no explanation. Offering ourselves to the Lord every day in service – even sacrificial service, so that our lives are subordinated to His and He may truly live in us and His love may flow out through us to others – thus revealing Him to a world that desperately needs Him.

That is true worship.

The sermon

The sermon can often contribute to the overall sense that a service is something that must engage and entertain the congregants – with humour often being an important ingredient.

For all the reasons previously stated, far too many Christians remain spiritually immature and thus, unknowingly, become the necessary targets of the Bible's words in Hebrews 5:12, *"In fact, though by this time you ought to be teachers, you need someone to teach you the elementary truths of God's word all over again. You need milk, not solid food!"*

The whole premise of this book is that even those who have been Christians for, potentially, decades, need to hear again the basics of the Gospel. Certainly, this is demonstrated in the content of many a sermon – it is milk, not meat! The problem is not because the preacher has discerned a need for the hearers to be re-taught the basics of our faith but because the preacher him/herself is unable, through lack of Biblical understanding, to preach a "meaty" message.

The system used by many churches involves a revolving list of speakers. This can result in the person tasked with filling the preaching slots inviting and accepting almost anyone and everyone – just to get that slot filled.

So, the Church is often presented with someone whose heart may be in the right place but who patently has not been equipped by the Lord for that task. It should be remembered that if the Lord has not equipped us for a task, then, we have only human strength and human wisdom on which to rely – and that brings no glory to the Lord. Everyone who stands up to share God's

Word should be able to start with, "I believe the Lord wants me to share this passage, this message, with you today..."

If that condition is met, it eradicates another error that the Church commits regarding preaching and that is, the time limit. Times may vary from church to church, but each church – and each congregant attending the individual churches – will know how long the sermon will last. How will they know that? They will know because, it is the same every week, and the timing is under human control, and not the control of the Spirit. If the message being presented is truly from the Lord it will have a beginning and end decided by the Lord, and discerned by the Spirit-appointed preacher. One week the message may last 15 minutes, the next week it may last an hour. But the Spirit is rarely, if ever, offered that freedom, and access to the Church.

Another error with most sermons is that many preachers are unable to define and separate teaching and preaching. So, some will, knowingly or otherwise, be seeking to teach within the sermon. The understanding that needs to be grasped by the Church in this regard is that the Sunday service is for the proclamation of the Word, and for the building up of the Church for the week to come. It is a time for reminding, encouraging, inspiring and strengthening those present through the life-changing basic truths of the Gospel. The message should be uncontroversial: it may be a challenge to individuals present but not seeking to impart new knowledge, and certainly not lifestyle focused. Christianity is not a self-improvement course, yet so many preaching messages are wrongly focused on how Christians can/should change/improve their lifestyle. The focus must be Christ.

If the Sunday message is used solely for teaching, the opportunity to remind, encourage, and uplift is lost for another week. Additionally, a "seeker" is more likely to attend a Sunday service than any other event, and a message that builds up the Christian will also meet the needs of the seeker.

Teaching is not proclamation and exhortation, as is preaching, it is the imparting of knowledge to others. This should not happen at a Sunday service or the encouragement, motivation, building up and empowerment available through proclamation will be lost to the congregants. Teaching should be reserved for separate occasions – an evening gathering, a house group meeting, a monthly event on a Friday, Saturday, or Sunday evening – and so on. Such a teaching meeting will, inevitably, be longer than a Sunday morning service (which is another reason for not trying to teach in a Sunday morning service). It will be "meat." It will move the Christian along in their Christian journey, or it may remind and encourage them as Peter wrote in 2 Peter 1:12, *"So I will always remind you of these things, even though you know them and are firmly established in the truth you now have."* It may be controversial, for it will be new knowledge and understanding for many present.

A Biblical command that is so often ignored by churches regarding teaching is, James 3:1: *"Not many of you should become teachers, brothers, because you know that we who teach will be judged more strictly."* Clearly a command of which much of the Church is either unaware or has chosen to ignore.

Another great error in the presentation of any message in a church is that such a presentation is almost always a monologue – the preacher preaches, the teacher teaches, and the congregation sits mute and listens. This is not the Biblical way. The Bible, when referring to the proclaiming of the Gospel within meetings, as well as in public places, in the times of the early Christian Church records that: Acts 9:29, Paul *"…talked and **debate**d with the Hellenistic Jews, but they tried to kill him."* Acts 17:17 says, *"So he **reasoned** in the synagogue with both Jews and God-fearing Greeks…"* In Acts 18:19, Paul, *"…went into the synagogue and **reasoned** with the Jews."* In Acts 19:8, *"Paul entered the synagogue and **spoke boldly** there for three months, **arguing persuasively** about the kingdom of God."* It wasn't just Paul, Acts 18:28 says of Apollos, *"For he **vigorously refuted** his Jewish opponents in **public debate**, proving from the Scriptures that Jesus was the Messiah."*

The very polite, but spiritually unhelpful way in which the Bible is preached and taught in modern times is not seen in the Scriptures. There are many other such examples in the New Testament, not least of which are the often fiery engagements between Jesus and those who sought to reject His teaching and preaching.

The idea of one person speaking to an audience for 20 minutes or more, with no opportunity for any interaction is not how preaching or teaching is supposed to be done. An accurate understanding of the Scriptures is more likely to be reached when those present can discuss, debate, question, express doubts, argue, and so on, with the speaker and with each other about the message that has been presented.

Of course, this could be unsettling and challenging for the speaker, and it might disrupt the tightly controlled schedule—but it would align the Church more closely with the biblical model, and almost certainly lead to deeper understanding and, in time, greater communal agreement on the Gospel message.

Communion/Breaking Bread

In most churches today, the breaking of bread has been taken over by the new priesthood. It has been turned into a ceremony full of rituals. In many churches, the ordinary Christian has been removed from any role, except receiving that which they are given. In almost all churches, it is an event that is restricted in time and frequency. There are churches that will not allow non-members to participate, while other churches have other restrictions. This is all a long way from what Jesus instituted and from what He told His followers to do.

So, a ritualistic ceremony, performed in a church, brief in the time allowed for it, often administered following a queuing process, or a kneeling and waiting process, and administered only to those who "qualify" by those who are "qualified" to so administer.

In Acts 2:42 the Bible says that the early Christians had four spiritual devotions, one of which was a devotion to breaking bread. The English Oxford Dictionary defines devotion as, "Enthusiastic addiction." In other words, it is not a compulsive addiction over which the addict has no control – it is an addiction about which the "addict" is enthusiastic.

Realistically, no church-going Christian today could claim an "enthusiastic addiction" to breaking of bread when it is held once a week, once a fortnight, or even once a month in church.

One of the purposes of the Israelites celebrating the Passover every year was to allow them to personally identify with their forebears and, more importantly, with God's act of saving grace at the first Passover.

It is the same with the modern-day breaking of bread. It is an opportunity for Christians to personally identify with God's act of amazing grace, the giving up of His Son for lost sinners. As the remembrance of the original Passover meal put the Israelites – spiritually and emotionally – back in Egypt on the night of the Passover, so the remembrance instituted during the Lord's last supper puts the Christian, spiritually and emotionally, back at the cross.

It is noteworthy that there are not very many mentions of breaking bread in the New Testament, and this is generally accepted as being because it was such a normal part of early Christian fellowship that it didn't warrant a special mention.

Acts 2:46, *"They broke bread in their homes and ate together with glad and sincere hearts."* There are no definite references to breaking of bread taking place within a formal, church setting. The original Passover meal was a family affair, Jesus instituted the Christian breaking of bread over a meal with disciples, and the early Christians broke bread within each other's homes either as part of or following a meal.

The Corinthian church (1 Corinthians 11) had moved the breaking of bread out of individual homes and into a communal meals setting in which they engaged, but this, Paul makes clear, had created problems because the "bring and share meal" had become a situation, (1 Corinthians 11:20-21), where human nature, including greed and selfishness, was prevailing, thus, rendering the breaking of bread pointless.

The importance of time

There are four aspects to breaking bread, and these are (1) a remembrance of salvation, (2) a reflection upon the cost of that salvation, (3) an opportunity to develop and strengthen unity, and (4) a reminder that Jesus is coming again.

(1 & 2) Salvation and the cost involved

Breaking of bread is an opportunity to remember what Jesus has achieved. Jesus' words, Luke 22:19, *"Do this in remembrance…"* are an invitation to experience the Christian's union with Christ in His death and resurrection. As well as remembering our union with Christ – through our death to sin, our baptism into Christ and our being raised through His resurrection into a new life – it is a time of celebrating that union. Acts 2:46-47 says: *"They broke bread in their homes and ate together with glad and sincere hearts, praising God and enjoying the favour of all the people."* Glad hearts and praising God: Remembrance and celebration; Well regarded by those outside the Christian community.

Breaking bread is an opportunity to remember the cost paid for the Christian's salvation. The early Christians ate together with *"…glad and sincere hearts"*– and that sincerity speaks of the reflection upon the cost. It is possible for a Christian to take their salvation lightly and not have their lives radically changed if they only celebrate their salvation and do not take time to reflect upon the cost. The time spent reflecting upon the cost of salvation can provide a powerful stimulus for each Christian to live more in their salvation.

(3) Develop and strengthen unity

The purpose of breaking bread is to bring the Christian back to the cross of Christ. It is at the cross that Christians stand most hope of achieving unity because the cross is the great leveller.

Unity requires humility, and the best place for a Christian to experience humility is at the foot of the cross. Unity is essential for the Christian witness. John 17:23 says, *"...so that they may be brought to complete unity. Then the world will know that you sent Me..."* and unity brings a greater power in prayer and enables the presence of the Lord as Matthew 18:19-20 says, *"I tell you that if two of you on earth agree about anything they ask for, it will be done for them by My Father in heaven. For where two or three gather in My name, there am I with them"*. This may explain the constant presence of the Lord amongst the early Christians.

(4) Reminder of the Second Coming

1 Corinthians 11:26 says, *"For whenever you eat this bread and drink this cup, you proclaim the Lord's death until He comes."* Breaking bread is a reminder of an unalterable future event, the coming again of the Lord Jesus. The early Christians lived with the constant expectation of the Lord's imminent return, and their lives reflected this. Living with a constant reminder of His coming again will affect the way Christians live their lives. Through allowing the breaking of bread to drift from the frequent, powerful spiritual experience that it once was, modern Christians have also drifted away from this constant expectation of Jesus' return and, therefore, the ability to live in a way that reflects that expectation.

Summing up...

Perhaps the clearest illustration of the benefit of re-establishing a Biblical approach to breaking bread is that found in Luke 24:13-31. It is the story of the disciples on the road to Emmaus. They were with Jesus, talking with Jesus, discussing the Scriptures with Jesus and their hearts were burning within them – yet it was not until they broke bread together, in their home, over a meal, that they recognised Jesus, and their lives were dramatically impacted by the Risen Christ.

To regain the powerful spiritual benefits that come through breaking bread, Christians need to have the Biblically based confidence to take it back from the priesthood, remove it from church, return it to family homes (and house groups etc) and allow sufficient time and frequency for what is a very significant, humbling, unifying and empowering act of remembrance.

The Collection

One of the objections that many people have against the Church is that, in popular perception, "They are always after your money." This was graphically demonstrated to me many years ago, back in the 1990's, when a colleague and I walked a 12ft high wooden cross from north London, through the centre of London and on to south London. We needed to move the cross anyway, and we thought that rather than hiring a van we would turn it into an opportunity to witness to the Gospel.

So, from Islington in the north, across London Bridge and the River Thames to Morden in the south, we spent the major part of the day walking – and talking to the countless people who engaged with us. One thing stood out very clearly through those engagements. It was that people were very happy to talk about spiritual matters – their personal beliefs, questions about Christianity, the merits of Buddhism and many other spiritual topics – but as soon as the topic turned to Church people switched off, attitudes changed, and conversations were terminated. It was very, very clear. Church is not popular with a significant number of people – despite their spiritual awareness and interest.

One of the two main problems expressed by those we spoke with was the perception that churches are "always after your money." This is easy to understand when most, even first-time visitors to a church, will at some point in the service have a receptacle placed in front of them and, very publicly, they will be expected (despite any words from the service leader to the contrary) to place some money into that receptacle.

Has the Church lost sight of God's promises of provision? David knew the faithfulness of God's provision when he wrote, Psalm 37:25, *"I was young and now I am old, yet I have never seen the righteous forsaken or their children begging bread.*" The Church should not be thrusting a receptacle in front of everyone who enters through their doors in the expectation that everyone will give money. The Lord will provide for all the needs of every faithful church.

George Mueller is still a relatively well-known figure amongst Christians. In the 19th century, he set up a ministry in the city of Bristol, England taking in many of the orphans who were living without any form of support. For this reason, many think that Mueller had a real heart for the orphans. Now, that may be true but what may not be so well known is that the plight of the orphans was not the motivation for Mueller's ministry. The orphans were the vehicle by which Mueller sought to demonstrate to an unbelieving Church that God provides for all our needs – the orphans' needs, and Mueller's needs within his ministry. And the Lord was, obviously, faithful to His Word.

In a significantly smaller ministry, I too have experienced the Lord's faithfulness in provision. In 1987, following a very clear call from the Lord, I moved from Devon in south-west England to London to start a ministry amongst the young homeless. The Lord provided, through a London-based minister I had come to know shortly before I moved to London, the initial accommodation I needed whilst I set about setting up the ministry.

A large, underused church then allowed me to use a significant portion of their building to house the young homeless and, in June 1988, I took in the first young, homeless person. From then until August 1999, when the ministry concluded, and without me ever asking anyone for anything, the Lord faithfully provided for all my needs and all the needs of the countless young people I took off the streets during that 11-year period. And not one of those young people was allowed to sign on for Government benefits (welfare) whilst they stayed with me. Everything we needed came from the Lord - accommodation, food, clothing, finances, and even cars and holidays.

Leaving the Lord in charge of the income, left Him in charge of the whole ministry – I could not carry it on unless God provided what we needed. The Church should similarly begin to trust the Lord for His provision. If the Lord's blessing is on a church, He will provide what is needed for them to continue, but if the church is wayward, with unbelieving clergy or leaders who do not meet the Bible's criteria, or who preach a message that is contrary to the Word of God, the Lord will not bless such a church and the needed provision will not come.

Does the Church have sufficient confidence that they are carrying out the Lord's will that they will hand the matter of provision over to Him?

Paul gives a clear instruction regarding collections. He writes in 1 Corinthians 16:1-3, *"Now about the collection for the Lord's people: Do what I told the Galatian churches to do. On the first day of every week, each one of you should set aside a sum of money in keeping with your income, saving it up, so that when I come no collections will have to be made. Then, when I arrive, I will give letters of introduction to the men you approve and send them with your gift to Jerusalem."*

The instructions are clear – give in accordance with income, save it up, no collections, give to those in need of the support.

Instead, we generally have a situation where a collection is made every Sunday in almost every church, it disappears off to a back office, with some denominations sending a chunk off to a central office, and much of it gets disposed of in ways of which the congregants are not informed – except in the vaguest of terms. Added to this, it was my experience whilst in ministry that most gave from their excess (not in accordance with their income), and very few gave sacrificially – not surprising when the Church does not preach a sacrificial Gospel and lifestyle.

Departure

The hour, or the hour and a half, is up. The service is ended. With the need for outward shows of piety removed, it is but minutes before the social chit-chat resumes. The children are released from Sunday School and let loose to run around the church, and teas, coffees, and biscuits are enjoyed by many.

There is no waiting upon the Lord, no healthy debates and discussions about the message of the sermon. The environment discourages private prayers or meditation.

The end of service and departure routine is as controlled as the service. If the Lord had turned up for the service, it is perfectly clear that, following whatever form of dismissal that occurs, the Lord's time is up!

The 20 minutes or so that are allowed for the social diehards passes, the stragglers leave, and the church closes for another week – except for the utterly predictable, timed and controlled house groups, coffee mornings, Mums & Toddlers, Pensioners' lunches, Teen Youth group and so on.

Truthfully analysing the service and the other weekly church activities, it is not hard to see how the church is transforming into, essentially, a social hub. Some may seek to justify that as outreach – but we have only to look at the declining influence of the Church and the Gospel within society to understand that this creeping transformation is having the opposite effect.

Pervading Evidence of Error

Lastly, a very common and sad illustration that the Church is off track – doctrinally and in its practices – is that the majority of those calling themselves Christians and attending church regularly go through their entire life without ever personally experiencing the Lord using them in any kind of supernatural way. Numberless multitudes of those to whom could be applied 2 Timothy 3:5, *"...having a form of godliness but denying its power."*

Deceived by the induced emotional highs created by what is wrongly called worship, and believing such emotional highs to be the work of the Holy Spirit, the vast majority of church attendees never experience the supernatural breaking through in the form of the laying on of hands for healing, the commanding of evil spirits to leave a person or location, the clearly answered prayers on a myriad of matters, a specific call to service, a Divine word of knowledge, a prophecy, the miraculous provision for individual needs, a Divine word of wisdom – and so much more.

With these gifts and others lying dormant and unused (or even misused), the Church and individual Christians are disqualified from taking the position occupied by Paul, who was able to declare, in 1 Corinthians 2:4, *"My message and my preaching were not with wise and persuasive words, but with a demonstration of the Spirit's power,"*

The Good News is that God hasn't changed and will not change. His message to the Church today is simple, Jeremiah 29:13: *"You will seek Me and you will find Me when you seek Me with your whole heart."*

Part Five:

The way forward

"As of first importance…"

Introduction

In the first section of this book, I presented an explanation as to how I believe the Church has come to be seen, by the general public, as powerless and irrelevant. In the second section I presented various fundamental doctrines which I believe the Church is currently, Biblically, getting wrong. In the third section, I presented some examples of well-known Bible passages whose true meanings have been lost to the Church, and therefore, to most church attendees. In the fourth section, I examined several Church practices that I believe, Biblically, the Church is also getting wrong.

As I bring the book to a close, the question may become – for those who accept what is presented within the book – "Where do we start?"

It will come as no surprise to find out that the Bible has presented us with an answer to that question. In applying that answer, the process of change can begin, confusion can be avoided, and unity can be built.

The Apostle Paul, in 1 Corinthians 15:1-11, outlines the things which are "…*of first importance*" to Christians, as individuals and as a Church. It is upon the issues which Paul covers in this passage in 1 Corinthians that there is no room for personal opinion. Understanding Paul's teachings in this passage, and applying them as he teaches, means the Church (or church) will change together, correct priorities will be maintained, and divisions and splits can be avoided.

There is an ever-present need to hold to clear Biblical revelation and, as a Church, to unite around that revelation. It is upon the issues revealed in this passage that Christians should know what they believe and why they believe those things. The issues that Paul labels in 1 Corinthians 15 as being *"...of first importance"* are the very basics of the Christian faith.

If the Church will take hold of them, preach them and teach them, then far greater unity will be the result, a greater ability to evangelise will result, and Sunday morning services can concentrate on exalting the God who gave Himself for humanity, rather than on the perennial search for a new angle on a 2,000-year-old, very simple story.

1 Corinthians 15:1-11

1. Now, brothers, I want to remind you of the gospel I preached to you, which you received and on which you have taken your stand.

2. By this gospel you are saved, if you hold firmly to the word I preached to you. Otherwise, you have believed in vain.

3. For what I received I passed on to you as of first importance: that Christ died for our sins according to the Scriptures,

4. that He was buried, that He was raised on the third day according to the Scriptures,

5. and that He appeared to Peter, and then to the Twelve.

6. After that, He appeared to more than five hundred of the brethren at the same time, most of whom are still living, though some have fallen asleep.

7. Then He appeared to James, then to all the apostles,

8. and last of all He appeared to me also, as to one abnormally born.

9. For I am the least of the apostles and do not even deserve to be called an apostle, because I persecuted the church of God.

10. But by the grace of God I am what I am, and His grace to me was not without effect. No, I worked harder than all of them - yet not I, but the grace of God that was with me.

11. Whether, then, it is I or they, this is what we preach, and this is what you believed.

In 1 Corinthians 15:1-11 there are six doctrinal issues which Paul highlights as being, "*…of first importance…*" They are:

1. Verses 3 & 4: "*…according to the Scriptures…*"

Biblical revelation is the basis of Christian faith.

2. Verse 3: "*…Christ died for our sins…*"

Forgiveness of sins through Christ's death,

3. Verse 4: "*…raised on the third day…*"

Justification,

4. Verse 5: "*…He appeared to…*"

 Assurance of faith,

5. Verse 9: "*…I…do not even deserve…*"

Undeserved grace,

6. Verse 10: "*…His grace…was not without effect…*"

Empowering grace.

An overview shows that Paul considers it of first importance for Christians that all doctrine must be grounded in Scripture. Forgiveness of sins through Christ's death is the basis of a Christian's relationship with God and so a foundational truth of the Christian faith. Christian justification is, Biblically, based upon the resurrection of Christ and this is a third foundational truth of Christianity. Paul highlights the Word of God, the cross, and the empty tomb as the first three foundations of Christianity.

Based on these, Paul then highlights Christ's many post-resurrection appearances as a way by which Christians may have an assurance of what they believe. Paul then declares, as a foundational truth, that the grace extended by God to humanity is entirely undeserved, but goes on to point out, as the last foundational truth of Christianity, that receiving grace is the way to empowerment within the life of a Christian.

1. "...according to the Scriptures..."

It is important for Christians to understand that Christ's life, death and resurrection were all in fulfilment of Scripture. God's plan for the salvation of humanity, through His Son, is outlined in Scripture from Genesis 3 onwards. In Luke 24:27, when the post-resurrection Jesus was on the Emmaus Road with two disciples, He explained to them all the events that had just occurred, involving Himself, in Jerusalem *"...beginning with Moses and all the Prophets."*

The early disciples certainly knew the importance of a faith that rested on Biblical revelation, rather than only on experience or someone else's teaching. In Acts 17 is the account of the Apostle Paul in Thessalonica. He went to the synagogue and, with the Jews there, he (verses 2-3), *"...reasoned with them from the Scriptures, explaining and proving that the Christ had to suffer and rise from the dead."* Another example of this Scriptural foundation for the Christian faith is in Acts 8 when Philip explains the Good News about Jesus to the Ethiopian eunuch. In Acts 18:28, it tells of Apollos, an early convert who, *"...vigorously refuted the Jews in public debate, proving from the Scriptures that Jesus was the Christ."* Jesus repeatedly told His disciples and others that His life, death and resurrection were to be in accordance with Scripture (Matthew 26:54. Mark 14:49, John 5:39 and others).

Every Christian should desire to understand Scripture so deeply that, when confronted with the widespread false teachings of today—those that challenge core tenets of the faith such as the virgin birth, the bodily resurrection of Jesus, the assurance of salvation, and other foundational truths—they, like Apollos, can vigorously refute error and demonstrate from the Scriptures that Jesus is the Christ. A better understanding of the Scriptural revelation of salvation will strengthen each Christian's understanding of how salvation is entirely a work of God for humanity and, thus, clear up much of the confusion that exists today about a Christian's role in their salvation.

2. "...Christ died for our sins..."

This is the second foundational truth of the Christian faith which Paul lists as being *"...of first importance."* Two thousand years after Christ's death and resurrection, there is a great deal of confusion within the Christian Church about how and when a Christian's sins are dealt with. This confusion often adversely affects the day-to-day relationship which many Christians have with God. Within the Church today there are those who are expecting to be judged when they meet with God at the end of their time on earth. There are Christians who have an underlying nervousness, even fear, at the thought of that encounter with God. The Catholic Church has come up with the doctrine of purgatory which specifically lays the punishment for some of their sins upon the Catholic individual. Some Christians believe that God is less pleased with them, less close to them, and less likely to bless them after they have sinned. Some Christians believe that their sins are dealt with by God as and when they occur and as and when forgiveness is requested. Yet the Scriptures say, *"Christ died for our sins."*

Isaiah 53 makes it quite clear that Christ bore the sins of every person into Himself and, also, bore the punishment for those sins. This truth is the very basis of the Good News, but it has become obscured by wrong teaching and, in Paul's day as now, there is a need to clearly proclaim the Good News that *"Christ died for our sins."* When John the Baptist saw Jesus, he declared, *"Look, the Lamb of God who takes away the sin of the world."* (Jn 1:29). Jesus Christ has taken away the sins of not only the Christian but of everyone in the world (1 John 2:2). The only issue outstanding between God and humanity is acceptance or rejection of His Son (John 3:18 and others). Yet, so many are taught that their sins are still an issue between them and God.

Bible teachers get their listeners to go through antics such as writing their "sins" on a piece of paper and then putting them into a bin as though this symbolised getting rid of the sin; another role-play is to write the troublesome "sin" on a balloon and then release the balloon into the air - again symbolising the letting go of that sin. This dangerous form of teaching, which has been quite widespread in its various forms, is in error in three major areas; firstly, it suggests that sin is still an issue between God and man - contrary to the revelation of Scripture; secondly, sin has still to be dealt with as it occurs - again, contrary to Scripture and, thirdly, it suggests that the Christian plays some part in getting rid of their sin, which is also contrary to Scripture. It may seem a harmless exercise to go through such a role-play, but it is undermining the most basic truth of the Christian faith, that *"…Christ died for our sins."*

The Good News of the Gospel is that Christ died for our sins whilst we were still sinners (Romans 5:8). God did not wait for a person to make every effort against sin before He made that person acceptable to Himself through Christ. Equally, now the Christian has been made acceptable, God makes no demand that the Christian makes every effort against sin and so take on a heavy burden (see: Matthew 11:30) because He has dealt with everyone's sins. Romans 6:10 confirms that Jesus, when He died for our sins, *"...died to sin once for all..."* Jesus died once and He died for all. Let the Christian rejoice at the Good News, that *"Christ died for our sins"* and that in so doing, He dealt with sin for all time for all people. Let every Christian be assured that forgiveness of sins comes through the death of Christ and the death of Christ alone. That forgiveness cannot be added to nor taken away from. The Christian stands forgiven because *"Christ died for our sins."*

3. "...raised on the third day..."

Paul goes on to write, in the passage being examined, that Jesus, *"...was raised on the third day according to the Scriptures..."* In Romans 4:25, it says of Jesus that, *"He was delivered over to death for our sins and was raised to life for our justification."* The death of Christ, taking away all sin and all punishment for sin from the Christian, lays the foundation for a new relationship with God. The resurrection of Christ, assuring the Christian's justification, maintains an ongoing relationship with God. Justification moves the Christian into the position of being, from God's perspective, as though they had never sinned. Once again Paul makes the point that this happened according to the Scriptures. Psalm 16:10, amongst others, contains a prophecy that Christ would rise from the dead. Paul quotes that particular Scripture in Pisidian Antioch, in Acts 13, and Peter refers to it in his address at Pentecost in Acts 2. The very exciting and Good News about the resurrection, apart from the fact that it means justification for the Christian, is that - as this is the means of Christian justification - it puts the responsibility for Christian justification squarely onto God and the Bible teaches that God accepted that responsibility because, in Romans 1:4, it says that Jesus was raised from the dead by the Spirit of Holiness.

So far in this passage, Paul has revealed, through foundational truths of the Christian faith that doing away with sin is entirely God's responsibility and justification of the Christian is, also, entirely God's responsibility. This is the very Good News of the Gospel. It allows no room for the doubts and fears that assail so many Christians through a lack of knowledge of the basics of their faith. Romans 5:18 also points the Christian to Christ as the means of justification. It says, *"...the result of one act of righteousness was justification that brings life for all men."* The Scriptures speak repeatedly (Romans 3:24, 3:26, 5:1, 5:18, 1 Corinthians 6:11, Galatians 3:24, Titus 3:7 amongst others) of how the Christian is justified by grace, through faith. Sending Jesus to bear the punishment due to sin was God's act of grace to humanity. The Christian's God-given faith in Christ's resurrection provides for their justification. This means the day-to-day position of the Christian before God is entirely unaffected by the daily living of that Christian - and that's Good News!

4. "...He appeared to..."

Christianity is not a religion of blind faith. In Acts 1:3, it says that after His resurrection, Jesus appeared to His followers *"...and gave many convincing proofs that He was alive."* Amongst the convincing proofs are His appearances, as listed in 1 Corinthians 15, to Peter, then the twelve Apostles, then to a gathering of more than five hundred of His followers, then to James, then to all the Apostles and, finally, to Paul. These appearances, excluding that of Paul, took place over a period of forty days. They occurred in different places and involved hundreds of different people. During the appearances, Jesus gave other proofs that He was alive. In Luke 24:39 Jesus invites the frightened disciples, who think they are seeing a ghost, to touch Him and to feel His flesh and bone. He invites them to look at the wounds He carries from the crucifixion. He then ate some food with them to further prove that He was alive and not an apparition. When Jesus appeared to the disciples on another occasion (John 20:27), He invited Thomas to touch the nail marks in His hand and to put his hand into the spear wound in Jesus' side.

Christianity is a religion that rests very much on firm evidence. Many people have set out, through the years, to disprove Christianity; but, as an American lawyer (Josh McDowell) discovered when he tried to disprove Christianity, there is enough evidence to prove in any fair court of law that Jesus Christ is exactly who He claimed to be. Christians are not supposed to live with doubts about the basics of their faith. In Hebrews 10:22, it encourages Christians to *"...draw near to God with a sincere heart in full assurance of our faith."* Full assurance! Any Christian having doubts should confront those doubts, following the example of Scripture. Many times, people came to Jesus with their doubts: Satan said to Jesus, *"If you are the Son of God..."*; a leper came to Him and said, *"If you are willing..."*; Peter said to Jesus, when He was walking on water, *"If it is You...."* it is not wrong to have doubts, but it is foolish to live with those doubts rather than confront them. Christians are encouraged to live, knowing the many convincing proofs that Jesus gave to His followers - and still gives today to His followers - in full assurance of their faith. This is not a side issue, it should be remembered that it is one of the truths which is of first importance. A Christian with doubts is a far less effective witness than a Christian who does have that full assurance of faith.

5. "...I...do not even deserve..."

Paul recognised, and freely confessed, that he did not deserve to be called an Apostle. He was one of the main persecutors of the fledgling Christian church. He calls himself, *"...the least of the Apostles."* Paul, though, does not stop with this confession of unworthiness. He goes on to say, *"But by the grace of God I am what I am."* This is the same attitude shown by the Prodigal Son, in Luke 15, when he returns home and is offered the undeserved love of the father he has wronged. In verse 21 of that chapter, the son says, *"Father I have sinned against heaven and against you. I am no longer worthy to be called your son."* Having recognised and confessed his unworthiness, the son then goes on to receive the gifts of love, and the restoration to the position of sonship, which the father freely offers him. Both Paul and the Prodigal Son demonstrate an important principle of grace, which is that it is extended to those who are undeserving and that to receive it is a positive choice made by the recipient.

This is the situation in which every human being finds themself. No one is worthy of the gracious gift of Jesus and all that flows through Him. Every Christian, though, needs to adopt the same position as Paul and say, *"I do not even deserve...but...."* For example, "I do not even deserve to be called a child of God, but by the grace of God I am what I am." Recognizing that no one deserves grace is what enables the Christian to freely receive it—and that is precisely what preserves its nature as grace. It will stop the Christian from falling into the trap of striving to, in some way, be worthy of the mighty gift of Jesus and all the grace that flows through Him. Grace is extended by God to humanity without regard to conditions or response. Paul understood that, received grace and went on to serve the Gospel in a mighty way. This truth of undeserved grace is very rightly included in those that Paul considers to be of first importance.

Two great problems weaken the Christian Church today, and both are covered by Paul's listing of the truths of first importance. The first great weakness from which the modern Church suffers is that the majority of Christians do not really know the Scriptures in the way they need to. They may be read, listened to and even learned; but there is a great lack of study and understanding - hence, superficial, traditional and even incorrect interpretations are accepted. The second great weakness of the Christian church today is its inability to accept God's freely offered grace. Bible teacher after Bible teacher, preacher after preacher, will encourage Christians to hold back from embracing grace in all its fullness, for fear that it may lead to license. Yet, in the verse under discussion, Paul declares that it is the grace he has received which makes him the person he is, and it is the receiving of grace that empowers every Christian to become the person they can be in Christ. In the Bible, Christians are called children of God, brothers of Jesus, Ambassadors of Christ and many other glorious names - none of them are deserved. All are positions freely offered.

6. "...His grace...was not without effect."

Paul received grace which, although he didn't deserve it, was freely offered to him - as it is to every Christian and, indeed, every human being. Paul goes on in this passage to write that in the receiving of grace, he was empowered to work harder than any of the others in the church. Paul is teaching here a truth "*...as of first importance*" that is not understood by many Christians today and, indeed, is mistaught by the majority of Christian leaders, speakers, preachers and teachers. The truth is that, far from being an easy option or an alternative to obedience, grace is the very source of empowerment, service and obedience within the life of a Christian. It was not himself, declares Paul, but grace within him that produced all the hard work. What a great day for the Church when Christians stop trying to do so much for God and allow God, "*...who works in you to will and act according to His good purpose*" (Phi 2:13), to freely have His way. Colossians 1:6 tells what will happen in such an event. *"All over the world this Gospel is bearing fruit and growing, just as it has been doing among you since the day you heard it and understood God's grace in all its truth."* Gospel growth and fruit-bearing are assured - once the Christian understands grace. This is because that Christian will then be in the position of Paul and will allow grace to produce hard work for the Gospel - rather than striving to produce such work in human strength.

Receiving grace also empowers personal growth. Romans 5:17 says, *"...how much more will those who receive God's abundant provision of grace and of His gift of righteousness reign in life through the one man, Jesus Christ."* Receiving grace will empower the Christian to the point where they will reign in life - that is the Word of God. Grace is only ever taught in the Bible in the context of being a source of empowerment. How far these truths are from the fearful modern teachings that link abundant grace with a descent into license? Those who teach that Christians should beware of abusing grace or should hold back from embracing grace "too much," demonstrate by such teaching their lack of understanding of the Bible's teaching on the matter. Let every Christian embrace grace wholeheartedly and let such Christians know the empowerment that grace brings. Let every Christian declare to Christians and non-Christians alike, "By the grace of God, I am what I am."

Conclusion

When the Apostle Paul preached the Gospel, he did so, according to his testimony in 1 Corinthians 1:17, *"...not with words of human wisdom, lest the cross of Christ be emptied of its power."* Paul did this because, as he said earlier in the same verse, that is what Jesus sent him to do. Christians have been blessed with a Gospel that is not only Good News but is also very simple to understand. There may be a myriad of peripheral issues, but at the heart of the Gospel, there are just six foundational truths which every Christian should know and live by.

The truths of the Christian Gospel which the Bible declares to be *"of first importance"* are:

> **1.** That all that is revealed in the life, death and resurrection of Christ happened according to the Scriptures.

> **2.** That sin has been dealt with, once and for all, because Christ died for our sins that He might *"...give repentance and forgiveness of sins"* to the Christian (Acts 5:31).

> **3.** That Christ rose again on the third day and by that the Christian is forever justified.

4. That Jesus *"...gave many convincing proofs that He was alive"* (Acts 1:3) and that, therefore, the Christian may have *"...full assurance of faith"* (Hebrews 10:22).

5. That grace is never deserved and that to receive it, or not, is a choice made by each person.

6. That grace is the source of power in a Christian's life - not an alternative to obedience.

This is the Gospel of Christ. This is the *Good* News!

About
Kharis Publishing

Kharis Publishing, an imprint of Kharis Media LLC, is a leading Christian and inspirational book publisher based in Aurora, Chicago metropolitan area, Illinois. Kharis' dual mission is to give voice to under-represented writers (including women and first-time authors) and equip orphans in developing countries with literacy tools. That is why, for each book sold, the publisher channels some of the proceeds into providing books and computers for orphanages in developing countries so that these kids may learn to read, dream, and grow. For a limited time, Kharis Publishing is accepting unsolicited queries for nonfiction (Christian, self-help, memoirs, business, health and wellness) from qualified leaders, professionals, pastors, and ministers. Learn more at: https://kharispublishing.com/

www.ingramcontent.com/pod-product-compliance
Lightning Source LLC
Chambersburg PA
CBHW051425090426
42737CB00014B/2831